The Seven-Year-Old Wonder Book

For everyone who has ever been seven years old
or is,
or soon will be.

Isabel Wyatt

The Seven-Year-Old Wonder Book

Floris Books

Illustrations by Alyson MacNeill

First published by in 1958
This edition published in 1994 by Floris Books

British Library CIP Data available

ISBN 0-86315-527-8

Printed in Great Britain
by BPC Wheatons, Exeter

Contents

Sylvia and the Sick Toys

Sylvia lived with her mother in a white cottage at the edge of a dark wood. There was a nut-hedge round the garden, and in this hedge was a tall tree which Sylvia loved to climb.

One stormy afternoon she was riding a high branch, shouting as the wind rocked her, when suddenly there was a loud crack, and Sylvia found herself falling — falling — falling — crashing through the boughs below, which spread their arms to catch her, and passed her down from one to another till the lowest of all laid her trembling on the grass.

Sylvia wanted to cry; but she felt that would be ungrateful when the tree had tried with all its arms to save her. So she thanked the tree as bravely as she could, and limped indoors to her mother.

And her mother gently washed the scratches on her knee, and put some sweet-smelling rose-coloured ointment on, and bound it up with a soft white bandage, till Sylvia felt better there than anywhere else all over.

Now some of Sylvia's toys had had accidents, too. Pip, her red velvet dog, had wagged his tail off; Bruno, her brown bear, had lost an eye; and Jumbo, the father elephant, had sprained his trunk. Titania, her fairy doll, had torn her wings on a bad-tempered nail; Goldilocks' eyelids had got stuck wide open, so that she could not get a wink of sleep; and Kate, who was rather an elderly baby, had dripped her sawdust stuffing till she was nothing but skin and bone.

So Sylvia sat them in a row, and gently washed the sick

places, and put some sweet-smelling rose-coloured ointment on, and bound them all up with a soft white bandage, till they too felt better there than anywhere else all over.

Sylvia asked her mother:

"How soon shall we all be better, Mother?"

And her mother replied:

"As soon as you wake in the morning, Sylvia, if you go to the fountain of dew tonight, like the crippled wood-maiden."

Then Sylvia begged:

"Oh, Mother, do tell us about her!"

And her mother promised:

"Tonight, then, in bed."

So at bedtime, when Sylvia and Pip and Bruno and Jumbo and Titania and Goldilocks and Kate had crowded under the eiderdown together, Sylvia's mother sat at the foot of the bed and told them the Story of the Crippled Wood-Maiden.

And this is it:

The Story of the
Crippled Wood-Maiden

There was once a crippled wood-maiden, who lived all alone in an ivy house in the middle of a forest, for she had fallen out of a tree and hurt herself, and so she could no longer run and dance with the other wood-maidens.

One black and stormy night, a knock came at her door. She felt a little frightened; but she bravely opened the door, and there in the dark and rain stood a little old woman, all blown about and wet through.

The wood-maiden was so sorry for her that she quite forgot about being frightened; she took her by the hand, and brought her in, and dried her clothes, and made her comfortable by the fire, and brought her some strawberries and milk.

When the little old woman had eaten the strawberries and drunk the milk, she asked:

"If you could have a wish, dear child, what would it be?"

And the crippled wood-maiden answered:

"Oh, little mother, to be able to run and dance again with the other wood-maidens."

Then the little old woman said:

"Because you have been brave and opened the door although you were frightened, and because you have been kind to an old woman, I will tell you how to make your wish come true. In the Land of the Singing Sky there is a fountain of dew; and to sip one drop of it would make you well again."

The crippled wood-maiden sighed with joy at the thought; and she asked:

"Where *is* the Land of the Singing Sky, little mother?"

And the little old woman replied:

"At the top of the silver ladder which hangs from the full moon."

The crippled wood-maiden thanked her very happily, and piled fern and heather in the corner to make a bed for her. But when she turned round, there was no longer any little old woman to be seen.

As soon as the moon was full, the crippled wood-maiden went through the forest to the foot of its silver ladder. And there she found a beautiful lady, who smiled at her and asked:

"What are you seeking, little wood-maiden?"

And the crippled wood-maiden answered:

"Please, I have come to climb the silver ladder to the

Land of the Singing Sky, to sip one drop of the fountain of dew, to make me well again."

Then the beautiful lady said:

"But don't you know, little wood-maiden, that you can only do that if you bring six others with you?"

So the crippled wood-maiden went away; and on the trunks of the big trees at the four corners of the forest she wrote that if anyone needed making well again they should come to her ivy house before the next full moon.

But the days went by, and the nights went by, and nobody came, till at last there were only seven nights left till the moon would be full again.

That night there came a knock at the door; and when the wood-maiden opened it, outside stood a lion-cub with one paw festering from a thorn.

And the wood-maiden said:

"Come in, you poor lion-cub, and stay with me till the moon is full; and then we can both go and sip one drop of the fountain of dew together."

So the lion-cub came in thankfully.

The second night there came a knock at the door; and when the wood-maiden opened it, outside stood a honey-bear with his nose sore and swollen where the bees had stung him.

And the wood-maiden said:

"Come in, you poor honey-bear, and stay with lion-cub and me till the moon is full; and then we can all three go and sip one drop of the fountain of dew together."

So the honey-bear came in thankfully.

The third night there came a knock at the door; and when the wood-maiden opened it, outside stood a little black boy with his arm in a sling.

And the wood-maiden said:

"Come in, you poor little black boy, and stay with honey-bear and lion-cub and me till the moon is full; and then we can all four go and sip one drop of the fountain of dew together."

So the little black boy came in thankfully.

The fourth night there came a knock at the door; and when the wood-maiden opened it, outside stood a white swan with a dragging wing.

And the wood-maiden said:

"Come in, you poor swan, and stay with black boy and honey-bear and lion-cub and me till the moon is full; and then we can all five go and sip one drop of the fountain of dew together."

So the white swan came in thankfully.

The fifth night there came a knock at the door; and when the wood-maiden opened it, outside stood a tiny green lizard with only a stump where his long tail should have been.

And the wood-maiden said:

"Come in, you poor lizard, and stay with swan and black boy and honey-bear and lion-cub and me till the moon is full; and then we can all six go and sip one drop of the fountain of dew together."

So the tiny green lizard came in thankfully.

The sixth night there came a knock at the door; and when the wood-maiden opened it, outside stood a dwarf with one foot all wrapped up in bandages.

And the wood-maiden said:

"Come in, you poor dwarf, and stay with lizard and swan and black boy and honey-bear and lion-cub and me till the moon is full; and then we can all seven go and sip one drop of the fountain of dew together."

So the dwarf came in thankfully.

And now with the wood-maiden in the little ivy house were all the six others who needed making well again.

But the seventh night, the night before full moon, there came again a knock at the door; and when the wood-

13

maiden opened it, outside stood a water-nixie with a wound in her throat where a sword-fish had attacked her.

The wood-maiden stood silent a moment, for the water-nixie would make one too many; but she felt so sorry for her that she could not bear to turn her away.

So she said to her also:

"Come in, you poor water-nixie, and stay the night with dwarf and lizard and swan and black boy and honey-bear and lion-cub and me; and tomorrow, when the moon is full, we can all eight go and *try* to sip one drop of the fountain of dew together."

So the water-nixie came in thankfully.

The next night the moon was full, and they all went together through the forest to the foot of its silver ladder; and there they found the beautiful lady. One by one she helped them up the silver rungs; and at the top they came to the Land of the Singing Sky.

Very soft and low, from every side, there came the sweetest singing they had ever heard. Stars were growing in the fields there as thick as flowers in the fields below; and every star was singing. And singing children were flying among the stars on rosy wings.

And as the wood-maiden looked at them, she thought:

"Oh, if only *I* could fly among the stars like that!"

The beautiful lady led the way to the fountain of dew, and she said to the wood-maiden:

"Hold out your hands, little wood-maiden, and catch the rainbow-coloured spray."

So the wood-maiden cupped her hands and held them towards the fountain of dew; and seven drops of the rainbow-coloured spray fell into them.

Then the beautiful lady said:

"You may only have seven drops. But there are eight of you. Which one is to go without?"

Then the wood-maiden looked round slowly at them all

— at the water-nixie with the wound of the sword-fish in her throat; at the dwarf with his bandaged foot; at the tiny green lizard in such need of a new tail; at the white swan with her dragging wing; at the little black boy with his arm in a sling; at the honey-bear with his huge, sore, swollen nose; at the lion-cub with his festering paw.

And she felt there was not one of them she could deny a drop from the fountain of dew.

So she sighed, and turned to the beautiful lady, and said:

"I will go without myself."

Then she held out her cupped hands to the water-nixie. And the water-nixie sipped one drop; and at once the wound in her throat was well again. And the water-nixie thanked her.

Then she held out her cupped hands to the dwarf. And the dwarf sipped one drop; and at once his smashed foot was well again. And the dwarf thanked her.

Then she held out her cupped hands to the tiny green lizard. And the tiny green lizard sipped one drop; and at once he grew a fine new tail. And the tiny green lizard thanked her.

Then she held out her cupped hands to the white swan. And the white swan sipped one drop; and at once her dragging wing was well again. And the white swan thanked her.

Then she held out her cupped hands to the little black boy. And the little black boy sipped one drop; and at once his broken arm was well again. And the little black boy thanked her.

Then she held out her cupped hands to the honey-bear. And the honey-bear sipped one drop; and at once the stings stopped smarting, and his huge, sore, swollen nose was the size a honey-bear's nose ought to be again. And the honey-bear thanked her.

Then she held out her cupped hands to the lion-cub. And the lion-cub sipped one drop; and at once the thorn came out and his paw was well again. And the lion-cub thanked her.

Then she looked inside her hands; and they were quite empty. But the beautiful lady, standing close to the fountain of dew, called to her:

"Little wood-maiden, come and dance with me!"

And the wood-maiden answered sadly:

"I cannot dance. I am a cripple."

But the beautiful lady coaxed her again:

"Come and try!"

So the crippled wood-maiden came towards her, and took the hand which she held out; and the rainbow-coloured spray from the fountain of dew fell all about her, and she began to try to dance. And she found that she *could* dance; she could run and dance and leap just as she could before she fell out of the tree; she was no longer a cripple.

And when presently she stopped dancing, the water-nixie and the dwarf and the lizard and the swan and the black boy and the honey-bear and the lion-cub were no longer there. And the full moon and its silver ladder were no longer there, either.

And she cried:

"Oh dear, the silver ladder's gone! However shall I get down to my little ivy house?"

And the beautiful lady smiled and asked:

"Why not use your wings?"

And the wood-maiden looked behind herself, and she found that she too had rosy wings like the happy children she had watched.

And as she was spreading them the beautiful lady said:

"You can come every night to the fountain of dew, little wood-maiden. You do not need to wait for the full moon's silver ladder now you have found your wings."

So the wood-maiden flew happily down to her little ivy house, and folded her wings, and went in. And at sunrise she ran joyfully through the forest to join the other wood-maidens at their dancing once again.

The Poem of the Singing Sky

When the story was finished, Sylvia sighed and said:

"I wish *I* could fly about among the stars and hear them singing!"

And her mother answered:

"So you do — every night!"

And Sylvia said:

"Yes, but when I wake up I forget. I wonder if the Rhyme-Elves would paint a poem to remind me?"

For Sylvia had a Wonder-Book, in which the Rhyme-Elves painted poems for her in the night. Before she went to sleep, she would put the book on her bedside table, and chant a magic spell. And next morning, when she woke, there the book would be, open at a new page, and on the new page a new poem, beautifully painted in big letters, with a picture to go with it like the pictures in *this* book.

So now Sylvia reached under her pillow for her Wonder-Book, and placed it on the table. And when her mother had tucked her and all the sick toys snugly into bed, and said good-night, and gone quietly downstairs, Sylvia softly chanted her magic spell. And this was it:

> "Rhyme-Elves, rich in ringing words
> Won from winds and waves and birds,
> Lisping leaves and rustling rain,
> Sing — sing — for me again!"

As soon as she woke next morning she took off her

17

bandage, and she found that her knee was well again. Then she wakened the sick toys, and took off *their* bandages. And she found that Kate, the skin-and-bone baby, was quite plump again; and Bruno, the brown bear, had both eyes again; and Titania, the fairy doll, had new wings and could fly again; and Pip, the red velvet dog, could wag his tail again; and Goldilocks could go to sleep again; and Jumbo, the father elephant, could swing his trunk again ready for when any of his child-elephants needed spanking again.

So, hugging them all, and her Wonder-Book with them, Sylvia ran into her mother's room, and wakened her, and showed her all the sick places which had been made well again, and asked:

"Does that mean *we* found the fountain of dew last night, Mother, like the crippled wood-maiden?"

And her mother smiled, and answered:

"Of course you did!"

Then Kate and Bruno and Titania and Pip and Goldilocks and Jumbo and Sylvia all scrambled into Sylvia's mother's bed; and Sylvia opened her Wonder-Book at the new page, and together they all looked with joy at its two new pictures — a big coloured one of the crippled wood-maiden meeting the beautiful lady, and a small one of the wood-maiden, no longer crippled, marching happily into her little ivy house.

And then Sylvia's mother read them the new poem. And this is what she read:

> At night in bed I feel the windy beat
> Of rosy wings.
> The sky is filled with music soft and sweet,
> Which each star sings.
> Bright fields of singing stars go drifting by;
> And in them happy children sing and fly;

And with them — I.
I do not hear the singing stars by day,
Nor spread my wings.
I am too brisk and busy with my play
And waking things.
But music breathes again as night draws nigh,
Till flocks of children throng the singing sky,
And with them — I.

Sister-in-the-Bushes

As soon as Sylvia had dressed, she ran through the garden to her tall tree, and put her face among its leaves, and whispered:

"I found the fountain of dew in the night, so my knee's quite, quite better, thank you."

And, just to show the tree how well her knee was, she began to climb it again.

She was just reaching up to the bough from which she had fallen yesterday, reaching to pull herself up and astride it, when a soft voice murmured in her ear:

"Not *that* branch, Sylvia!"

And when Sylvia turned, there, just behind and above her, among the green leaves, stood a little girl in white, with golden hair so bright that it made Sylvia think of a candle-flame.

Sylvia stared and stared; and at last she gasped:

"Oh, *aren't* you lovely! Who are you, please?"

And the shining child replied:

"I am your sister."

Then Sylvia said:

"But you don't live with us."

And the shining child replied:

"No; I am your Sister-in-the-Bushes."

Then Sylvia asked:

"Won't you come and live with us in our white cottage? I've got a lovely mother."

And the shining child replied:

"I know — I have watched you together. But I don't want to live inside a house. I *like* living in the bushes."

Then Sylvia coaxed her:

"But if you came, then we could play together."

And the shining child replied:

"We can do that anyway. Whenever you want me, just part the bushes and call me, and I'll come."

Sylvia clapped her hands with joy at this; and then she asked:

"Sister-in-the-Bushes, how long have you lived in the bushes?"

And Sister-in-the-Bushes answered:

"As long as you have lived inside a house."

Then Sylvia asked again:

"Then why have I never seen you before?"

And Sister-in-the-Bushes answered:

"Perhaps because I'm shy. But today I forgot to be shy because you were in danger. Come and look!"

So Sylvia climbed up beside her, and from there she could see that the branch from which she had fallen yesterday was broken, and that if she had climbed astride it she would have fallen again. So she thanked Sister-in-the-Bushes for saving her today, and the tall tree all over again for saving her yesterday; and just then her mother called from the cottage door that breakfast was ready.

And as Sylvia ate her porridge and drank her milk she was bubbling with happiness; and she told her mother all about Sister-in-the-Bushes, and begged:

"I *may* play with her, mayn't I, Mother?"

And her mother answered, smiling:

"Of course you may."

Then Sylvia asked:

"Mother, did *you* have a Sister-in-the-Bushes, too?"

And her mother replied:

"Everyone has a Sister-in-the-Bushes, only sometimes they never find her. But she is always there, watching over them, like the Princess Helia with the Princess Gay."

And Sylvia cried:

"Oh, Mother, do tell me about them!"

And her mother promised:

"When bed-time comes."

When bed-time did come, Sylvia chose Titania, her fairy doll, to take to bed with her, because, although Sister-in-the-Bushes had no wings, and no magic wand with a star at the top, as Titania had, yet they reminded her a little of each other.

And this is the Story of the Star-Twins, which her mother told them when she had tucked them snugly into bed:

The Story of the Star-Twins

The Queen of the Stars was named Urania. She had many children, all born with a star upon their brow; but all except two had already grown up and left her palace to rule a star of their own. These two were twin daughters, called Princess Gay and Princess Helia. Gay was a strong, rosy, romping little princess, while Helia was pale and quiet; but each of them loved the other most dearly, and they could not bear to be parted even for a moment.

One day the romping Princess Gay said to the quiet Princess Helia:

"Helia, come with me to the Black Country!"

But the gentle Princess Helia shivered and exclaimed:

"Oh, Gay, *please* don't go to that terrible land!"

And Gay answered:

"But, Helia, I have set my heart on freeing its poor people from the Greedy Witch."

So the two star-princesses went to their mother and told her of Gay's wish. And Queen Urania said:

"It is right for Gay to go to the Black Country, to try to free the Greedy Witch's slaves. But Helia is too delicate to stand such harsh weather and rough ways. My dear daughters, the time has come when you will have to part."

The twin princesses were sad at the thought of parting. But Gay's longing to free the witch's slaves was so great that she knew that she must go. So one day she said farewell to her mother and her gentle sister Helia, and in her dress made out of starlight and with her star upon her brow, she set out on her journey, taking with her two coins of starry gold.

When she came to the shore of the Sea of the Nether Sky, she found a ship; and she asked the captain to take her across the sea to the Black Country; and she paid him with one of her two coins of starry gold.

While they were sailing, such a storm arose at midnight that the captain feared the ship would sink. But Princess Gay stood at the prow of the ship through the fiercest of the storm; and with the shining of the star upon her brow and of her dress made out of starlight, she guided the ship safely to the shore of the Black Country.

The Black Country was a bleak and gloomy land. The Greedy Witch made all the people go down into the mines to get precious stones for her. In the Cavern of Gloom, where she lived, she had tens of thousands and hundreds of thousands and thousands of thousands of jewels. But she was never satisfied. The more jewels her poor slaves found for her, the more she made them find.

When Gay began her journey across the Black Country, the Greedy Witch's slaves, with their black skins and their black cloaks and hoods and their weariness and their misery, could hardly stare enough at this shining princess in her dress made out of starlight and with a star upon her brow.

Some of them stared in joy and wonder; but some of

them tried to snatch away the star and the gleaming dress. So with her second coin of starry gold Gay bought a black cloak and hood, such as everyone wore in the Black Country; and she drew the cloak about her dress of starlight, and she drew down the hood over the star upon her brow, so that anyone meeting her now would never guess how beautiful she was inside.

So she journeyed safely on through the Black Country until at last she came to the Cavern of Gloom. As she groped her way inside, it grew darker and darker, till suddenly she turned a corner, and there before her sat the Greedy Witch, gloating over the enormous heaps of jewels which shone and flashed and sparkled and lit up the shadowy cave.

Now before Princess Gay had left her mother's palace, Queen Urania had taught her a magic word which would subdue the Greedy Witch. But the black cloak and hood which wrapped her about so closely had caused her to forget it. So when the Greedy Witch looked up and saw the star-princess standing there, it was she who spoke first; quickly she gabbled a spell which turned Gay into a small black spider.

And she drove the spider into a corner of the cave, crying harshly:

"Spin — spin — spin!
Grey miles of gossamer
To wrap my jewels in.
Do not from this corner stir.
Spin — spin — spin!"

Now in Queen Urania's palace among the stars there was a wonderful picture-gallery. On its walls, framed in gold, hung portraits of all the star-princesses and star-princes who were her children. When they were well and happy, their portraits smiled and sang; but if they were unhappy or in danger, their portraits wept.

Now the absent Princess Gay was always in Helia's thoughts; and three times every day she visited Gay's portrait to make sure that all was well with her. And at first the portrait smiled and sang; but one day she found it weeping.

Then Helia ran to Queen Urania, crying:

"Oh, Mother, something terrible has happened to Gay! I must go to her at once!"

And Queen Urania said:

"But, Helia, it would kill you to go to the Black Country!"

But Helia insisted:

"Not if I go to help Gay."

Then Queen Urania went quickly to Gay's portrait; and as soon as she saw it weeping, she said:

"The Greedy Witch has laid a spell upon her. Yes, Helia, you must go, for only you can set her free. But if you put on a black cloak and hood, you too will be lost; so I will give you instead a cloak and hood of dark blue air to cover your dress of starlight and the star upon your brow."

Then Queen Urania taught Helia the magic word which would subdue the Greedy Witch, and a second magic word which would release Gay from enchantment. And Helia said farewell to her, and set out on her journey, taking with her her cloak and hood of dark blue air and one coin of starry gold.

When she came to the shore of the Sea of the Nether Sky, she found a ship; but she was too shy to ask the captain to take her to the Black Country, so she laid her coin of starry gold on the deck, and floated up among the sails, wrapped in her cloak and hood of dark blue air.

While they were sailing, such a storm arose at midnight

that the captain feared the ship would sink. Then Helia cast off her cloak and hood, and stood at the top of the mast through the fiercest of the storm; and with the shining of the star upon her brow and of her dress made out of starlight, she guided the ship safely to the shore of the Black Country.

There Helia wrapped herself again in her cloak and hood, and swiftly and safely journeyed to the Cavern of Gloom. As she groped her way inside, it grew darker and darker, till suddenly she turned a corner, and there before her sat the Greedy Witch, wrapping her enormous heaps of jewels in grey miles of gossamer.

Then Helia threw off her cloak and hood; and the star on her brow blazed out, and her dress of starlight gleamed and glittered, till the light about her far outshone the light of all the witch's jewels.

The witch looked up in alarm; but before she could gabble her spell, Helia spoke out in a ringing voice the magic word which could conquer her. And at the sound of it the witch fell on her knees, and cringed, and cried for mercy.

Then Helia asked her sternly:

"Where is the star-princess whom you laid under a spell?"

And the kneeling witch pointed humbly to the corner in which a small black spider was spinning grey miles of gossamer.

Then Helia went to the corner and gently spoke the second magic word; and at the sound of it the small black spider turned into a star-princess, and the two sisters fell into each other's arms.

Then they set free all the slaves in the Black Country, and divided among them the jewels in the Cavern of Gloom. And the Greedy Witch begged humbly:

"Please take me back with you across the Sea of the

Nether Sky, that the Queen of the Stars may teach me how to become good."

So, taking the witch with them, they returned to Queen Urania's palace; and when she had heard their story, Queen Urania said:

"Never again need you be parted, my dear daughters, for I will give you twin stars to rule. And because you led the ships safely to shore, your twin stars shall do the same."

So the romping Princess Gay and the gentle Princess Helia were never again divided; and we can look up at the sky and see the stars they rule. And we call their stars the Heavenly Twins.

The Poem of the Black Cloak and Hood

Before Sylvia went to sleep, her mother held back the curtain and showed her the twin stars shining in the sky. Then Sylvia put out her Wonder-Book on the bedside table, and softly chanted her poetry spell:

"Rhyme-Elves, rich in ringing words
Won from winds and waves and birds,
Lisping leaves and rustling rain,
Sing — sing — for me again!"

When she woke next morning, the curtains were still closed; and in the half-dark she could see a star shining on the pillow beside her. When she jumped out of bed and climbed on the window-seat and drew the curtains back, she saw that this star was the star on Titania's magic wand, which Titania had moved a little in her sleep, so that it shone now on her forehead. And Sylvia stared at herself in the mirror, and thought:

"There's a star on *my* forehead, too, only my black hood covers it."

Then she turned to her open Wonder-Book; and she saw that on the new page there was a new poem, with a picture of Princess Gay guiding the ship through the storm. So she and Titania took the Wonder-Book into her mother's bed. And when they had looked happily at the picture, this is the poem her mother read to them:

When down to the dark Earth I sped
From where the stately stars are spread,
I set a black hood on my head.
But under it I still wear now
A secret star upon my brow.

In Earth's chill winds to keep me warm,
I wrapped a black cloak round my form.
But under it, where none can see,
My starlight dress still gleams on me.

Some day, shedding my dark disguise,
I shall shine starry as the skies,
And with my heavenly twin shall fare
Back to the home we used to share,
To rule twin stars together there.

The Making of the Fairy Tree

Sylvia was in the garden, helping her mother to gather the ripe seeds, when suddenly she stopped to ask:

"Mother, *how* can a big plant come out of this tiny seed?"

Sylvia's mother straightened her back and said, smiling:

"That's something Sister-in-the-Bushes might even *show* you!"

So Sylvia parted the bushes, and called down the slope:

"Please, Sister-in-the-Bushes, could you show me how a big plant comes out of this tiny seed?"

Then Sister-in-the-Bushes came out from among the leaves with a blue flower in her hand. And she answered:

"I'll try, Sylvia. Close your eyes!"

Sylvia closed her eyes, and Sister-in-the-Bushes touched them with the blue flower; and when she opened them, the ground had become as clear as glass, so that she could see deep down into it, and the stems of the plants had become fountains of green water, and the leaves were formed of green light, and from the flowers coloured flames were leaping. And everywhere the air was filled with floating rainbows, and tiny flashes of many-coloured lightning played round the bees and the butterflies.

Then Sister-in-the-Bushes called softly:

"Earth-Fairies, may Sylvia see you make a fairy tree?"

And out of the clear ground at Sylvia's feet came hurrying tiny knights in shining armour. They looked about, staring right through Sylvia; and their leader asked:

"But where *is* Sylvia? Oh dear, I suppose she's not seven yet?"

And Sylvia said:

"Not till New Year's Eve."

And he nodded his head, and said:

"We can't see little children till they're seven. But give me your seed, Sylvia. We can still show you how a fairy tree is made."

So Sylvia stooped and gave him her seed, and he laid it on the ground. Then all the tiny knights sank into the clear earth again, and lifted their hands, and called together:

"Sink down to us, little seed!"

And the seed sank slowly down into the earth to them, and a green fairy fire began to burn all round it, and a white root-tip appeared. And the little knights sank deeper still, and lifted their hands, and called together:

"Grow down to us, little root!"

And the white root stretched out, seeking its way down to them among the crystal stones; and they scooped up handfuls of milk from the clear earth, and gave it to the root to drink.

And as the root drank, a shoot peeped out from the top of the seed. And the tiny knights rose and clustered above it, and called together:

"Grow up to us, little shoot!"

And the shoot grew up through the clear earth, and came out into the light. On the surface of the ground it spread two leaves, and between them grew a straight green stalk.

Then Sister-in-the-Bushes again called softly:

"Dew-Fairies, may Sylvia see you make a fairy tree?"

Then the tiny mermaids who had been swimming in the dewdrops came gathering round the green stalk, and swam in and out about it, murmuring together:

"Grow upwards, little stalk, into the sunshine! Come out from the stalk, little leaves!"

And the stalk grew taller, and its leaves began to grow.

together, this was the new poem which Sylvia's mother
read to them:

> In leaf and stem, water;
> Earth in the root;
> Air in the blossom;
> Fire in the fruit.
> Fairies of Water,
> Fire, Air and Earth
> Ceaselessly toil that
> A plant may have birth.

The Dragon in the Sky

In another white cottage in another part of the dark wood lived Sylvia's friend, the Old Woodsman, all alone except for Blackbird, his black pony. Whenever Blackbird came by with a load of logs for the village, she would stop at Sylvia's cottage to take Sylvia, too. So when, the morning after Sylvia saw the fairy tree made, she heard *clop — clop — clop* along the woodland path, she cried eagerly:

"Oh, Mother, Blackbird's coming! May she take me for a ride?"

"And her mother answered:

"Yes, and will you ask Mr Woodsman nicely whether *we* may have some more logs, please? We shall soon need fires all day now autumn's here."

So Sylvia ran to the gate, and along came Blackbird with the resin-scented logs neatly piled in the cart behind her, and with the Old Woodsman striding beside her, looking made of love all over in his shabby corduroy trousers and his old, old hat. He took Sylvia up in his arms, and swung her on to Blackbird's back, and held her safe there with his huge strong hand. And Sylvia swayed gently with Blackbird's gentle movements, and listened with open ears and open eyes to the Old Woodsman talking, for there was nothing about the woods he did not know.

Today he said, in his slow, cosy voice:

"See how the leaves are turning yellow, Sylvia! Any day now, Knight Michael's wind will start blowing them away."

And Sylvia asked:

"Why is the wind Knight Michael's wind, Mr Woodsman?"

And he replied:

"Because it comes from the rushing of his sword as he fights the dragon. Didn't you know that every autumn, when the leaves turn yellow, Knight Michael fights the Dragon in the Sky?"

Sylvia was still thinking about this when Blackbird set her down again at the gate of her white cottage, and in the garden she found Sister-in-the-Bushes lying on the grass and staring at the wide, bright, empty sky. And Sylvia asked:

"Whatever are you staring at, Sister-in-the-Bushes?"

And Sister-in-the-Bushes answered:

"Close your eyes and come and see."

And she drew Sylvia down beside her, and touched her closed eyelids again with her blue flower.

And when Sylvia opened her eyes, everywhere about her she saw trails of blue and yellow mist; and out of the blue and yellow mist there loomed an enormous dragon, his long coils winding in and out among the tree-tops while his savage head reared right up into the sky. And across the sky towards him there came swiftly riding on a winged white horse a Knight in shining white armour; and his golden sword flashed like a sunbeam, and his cloak shimmered like moonlight as it streamed out behind him; and there was a great light on his brow.

And as he swung his sword, a strong wind began to blow, sweeping the leaves from the trees; and the dragon cowered, and drew back his head, and sank among the trailing mists.

When Sylvia went indoors to lunch, she told her mother all about what Sister-in-the-Bushes had shown her, and added:

"And I should have felt really frightened of the dragon, Mother, if Knight Michael had not been there."

And her mother answered:

"Yes, it is the dragon who always tries to make us

36

afraid, and it is Knight Michael's presence that makes us brave. That was what Snowflake found when *she* saw the dragon."

Then Sylvia coaxed:

"Oh, Mother, do tell me about Snowflake!"

And her mother promised:

"Tonight, then, in bed."

That night Sylvia chose Brian, her white toy pony, to take to bed with her, because, though he had no wings like the horse she had seen in the sky, she thought him very beautiful and quite swift and strong enough to be a brave knight's steed. And when Sylvia and Brian were snugly tucked into bed, Sylvia's mother told them this story of Snowflake and the Dragon:

The Story of Snowflake and the Dragon

One New Year's Eve the Queen of the Moon was making snowflakes. Her three little daughters caught them as they fell from her fingers, and they laid them in a boat of cloud; and when the boat was filled, they breathed on it and set it drifting down to Earth. And as the first boat sailed away, another floated towards them to be filled.

As they came to lay the snowflakes in the second boat of cloud, they all called out in wonder, for at the bottom of the boat there slept a tiny child, made out of snow.

And they all asked together:

"Oh, Mother, where is she going?"

The Queen of the Moon looked down at the Earth, and she told them:

"I can see a garden of lilies, and in the garden there is a

palace of crystal roofed with silver; and in the palace live a King and a Queen who are waiting for a little daughter. And this is the little daughter."

Then the first little princess said:

"Let us give her her name before she goes."

And the second little princess said:

"She is so white and small and lovely, she ought to be called Snowflake."

And the third little princess said:

"Yes, let us call her Snowflake."

They covered her gently with snowflakes, and then they breathed on the boat of cloud and sent it drifting down to Earth; and they stood quite still and quiet, and watched it as it floated further and further away.

As soon as it reached the Earth, it scattered its snowflakes over the waiting ground in a warm blanket, then went sailing on, bearing the sleeping child of snow into a rocky cave.

Now in this cave lived nine good fairies; and when they saw the gift which the boat of cloud had brought them they were very happy, and they laid Snowflake gently before their fire, and warmed milk from their fairy cows ready for her when she should awake.

And when Snowflake awoke, she looked round her at the bright, warm fire and at the bright, kind faces of the nine good fairies, and she asked:

"Who are you, please? And please, where am I?"

And the nine good fairies answered:

"We are the nine fairy mothers, and you have come from the Moon to stay with us in our cave for a little while."

So for nine months Snowflake lived in the cave with the nine fairy mothers, and each fairy mother in turn took care of her for a month while the others milked their fairy cows and made their fairy butter.

The first month, which was January, the first fairy mother took care of Snowflake, and gave her snow with her fairy milk.

The second month, which was February, the second fairy mother took care of Snowflake, and gave her dewdrops with her fairy milk.

The third month, which was March, the third fairy mother took care of Snowflake, and gave her tree-sap with her fairy milk.

The fourth month, which was April, the fourth fairy mother took care of Snowflake, and gave her leaf-buds with her fairy milk.

The fifth month, which was May, the fifth fairy mother took care of Snowflake, and gave her fruit-blossom with her fairy milk.

The sixth month, which was June, the sixth fairy mother took care of Snowflake, and gave her pollen with her fairy milk.

The seventh month, which was July, the seventh fairy mother took care of Snowflake, and gave her honey with her fairy milk.

The eighth month, which was August, the eighth fairy mother took care of Snowflake, and gave her barley with her fairy milk.

The ninth month, which was September, the ninth fairy mother took care of Snowflake, and gave her ripe red apples with her fairy milk.

And as soon as Snowflake tasted the ripe red apples, she longed to leave the cave and see what the outside world was like. So one day, when the ninth fairy mother was absent, fetching milk from the fairy cows, Snowflake began to creep along the narrow passage to where she could see the outer daylight shining. And when she reached the mouth of the cave, she saw that she was in a dazzling orchard, and in the middle of it stood an apple tree, laden with ripe red apples. And she ran to the apple tree, and picked an apple, and began to eat it.

But when she began to look for a way out of the orchard, she found there *was* no way, for a great Dragon had coiled his long body all the way round the orchard. And all the time he was coming nearer and nearer.

And the Dragon said:

"I am going to eat you, Snowflake!"

Then Snowflake began to tremble; and she ran back to the apple-tree in the middle of the orchard, and she cried:

"*Please* save me from the Dragon, Apple-tree!"

And the apple-tree bent down its highest branches, and lifted Snowflake right to the top of the tree.

But the Dragon said:

"Do not think you can escape me *that* way, Snowflake! I can reach you even there!"

And he still came nearer and nearer.

Then Snowflake looked to her right and to her left, and before her and behind her, but nowhere could she see any way of escape or anyone to save her.

Then the wind in the apple-boughs whispered:

"You have looked to your right and to your left and before you and behind you; but have you looked *upwards*, Snowflake?"

And when Snowflake looked upwards, she saw over her head a noble Knight in shining white armour riding swiftly across the sky on a winged white horse, and in his hand he held a glittering golden sword.

And Snowflake called out loudly:

"White Knight, *please* save me from the Dragon!"

Then the Knight looked down and saw her in the apple-tree; and he saw the Dragon coiling about its trunk and reaching up towards Snowflake; and he came riding swiftly down to Earth.

And at the wind of his coming, the Dragon looked up;

and then swiftly, swiftly, he began to uncoil himself from the trunk of the apple-tree; and he cried out very humbly:

"Do not slay me, Knight Michael, and I will fulfil my task."

Then Knight Michael asked sternly:

"What is that task?"

And the Dragon answered, still very humbly:

"It is to bring Snowflake safely to the garden of lilies, and to protect her while she lives upon the Earth."

Then Knight Michael looked up at Snowflake in the apple-tree, and he said:

"Come down from the apple-tree, Snowflake."

And Snowflake came down from the apple-tree very fearfully.

Then Knight Michael put his golden sword into her hand, and he said to her:

"If you thrust my sword into the Dragon's side and slay him, he will not defend himself while I am near. But if instead you lay my sword upon his head, he will ever after serve you faithfully. It is for you to choose, Snowflake, which thing you will do."

Then Snowflake looked at the Dragon, at his fanged jaws and hideous shape, and she shuddered and thought it would be better to slay him. Then she looked at his eyes, and they were so wistful and unhappy that suddenly she felt sorry for him.

So she came towards him, slowly and still a little fearfully. But the presence of Knight Michael gave her courage; and she stretched out her hand and laid the glittering golden sword on the Dragon's head.

And at once a faint, dull light began to shine forth from the Dragon, growing brighter and brighter until Snowflake saw that beneath his scales he had stars along his sides.

And now he looked so kind and friendly, and even beautiful with all his blazing stars, that Snowflake was no longer afraid of him, but seated herself upon his back quite trustfully.

Then Knight Michael received back his golden sword, and the Dragon brought Snowflake safely to the garden of lilies. And in the middle of the garden was a palace of crystal roofed with silver. And the King and Queen came out of the palace; and as soon as Snowflake saw them she loved them both, and she ran to them and was caught up into their arms.

So Snowflake became a princess, and lived happily with the King and Queen in the palace of crystal roofed with silver within the garden of lilies.

And the Dragon stayed with Snowflake to protect her all her life; and they became fast friends.

The Poem of Knight Michael

Before Sylvia and Brian went to sleep, Sylvia laid her open Wonder-Book on the table, and softly chanted her poetry spell:

> "Rhyme-Elves, rich in ringing words
> Won from winds and waves and birds,
> Lisping leaves and rustling rain,
> Sing — sing — for me again!"

And when she woke next morning, there was a new poem on a new page of the Wonder-Book, with a picture of Knight Michael on his winged horse riding towards the dragon, his cloak streaming behind him and his sword lifted high. And Sylvia bounced with excitement as she looked at it, for its portrait of Knight Michael's horse was exactly like Brian if only he had wings; and she wakened

43

Brian quickly to share in her excitement and pleasure about this portrait.

Then they took the Wonder-Book into her mother's bed; and this was the new poem her mother read to them:

Michael's sword
Is more burnished than a sunbeam;
Michael's mail
Is whiter than clear noon;
Michael's voice
Is majestic as the thunder;
Michael's cloak
Is brighter than the moon.
Michael's steed
Is swifter than a meteor;
Michael's brow
Is more radiant than the sky;
If my heart
Than the dragon's might is doughtier,
Michael's child
Am I.

Sylvia and the Old Woodsman

One afternoon a few days later, Sylvia heard the *clop —
clop — clop* of Blackbird on the woodland path, bringing
logs to her white cottage. She ran out and opened the gate,
and the Old Woodsman backed Blackbird carefully in; and
then came the part which Sylvia loved — climbing in and
out of the cart, unloading the logs, admiring their bark and
their rings and their grain and their scents and their
colours, and helping the Old Woodsman to carry them into
the wood-shed.

He piled them so beautifully, keeping oak and pine and
holly and hawthorn all separate, that Sylvia's love and
thanks brimmed over, and she cried:

"Oh, Mr Woodsman, you *are* so kind to us! *Why* are you
so kind to us?"

And the Old Woodsman straightened his backbone, and
pushed back his old, old hat, and looked down at Sylvia
standing looking up at him, and laughed his slow, cosy
laugh, and said:

"Well now, one beast *should* help another, as the Lowly
Ant said to the Lordly Cock!"

And as he went on working, Sylvia, as she went on
helping him, kept turning over his reply on her own
tongue:

"One beast *should* help another, as the Lowly Ant said
to the Lordly Cock!"

She thought it sounded magnificent; and she was quite,
quite sure there was a story in it somewhere.

So when they had finished stacking the logs, and had
given Blackbird her sugar, and had gone indoors and
washed, and the Old Woodsman was sitting by a fire of the

new logs while Sylvia's mother made tea, Sylvia came and stood between his knees, and looked up into his kind, brown face, and asked:

"Please, Mr Woodsman, why did the Lowly Ant say that to the Lordly Cock? Is it a story?"

And the Old Woodsman threw back his head and laughed his slow, cosy laugh, and picked Sylvia up and set her on his shiny brown corduroy knee; and she leaned back against his homespun coat, and loved to feel the tickling of its hairs and to smell its smell of trees and smoke and peat and woodland animals.

And the Old Woodsman said:

"Is it a story indeed! What a little greedy one you are for stories! All right — now just you listen, and I'll tell you!"

And in his slow, cosy voice that Sylvia loved, he told her the Story of the Lordly Cock. And I wish *you* could have been sitting on the Old Woodsman's knee and heard him telling it.

The Story of the Lordly Cock

There was once a Lordly Cock, a proud and mighty hero. One sunny morning he was strutting about the farmyard in his fine feather trousers, pecking at seeds and insects, when he came upon a Lowly Ant struggling with a seed much bigger than herself.

And Lordly Cock exclaimed:

"Oho, Lowly Ant! Now I can eat your seed and you as well!"

Now proud and mighty hero though Lordly Cock was, Lowly Ant was not the least bit afraid of him, but answered calmly:

"Do not eat my seed, mighty hero, for the ant-hill babies

need it. The ant-hill babies need me, too, so do not eat me either. Help me instead to carry the seed to them, for it is rather big for me to manage by myself."

This amused Lordly Cock, and he asked:

"Why should *I*, a mighty hero, carry the seed for *you*, a Lowly Ant?"

And Lowly Ant replied, as calmly as before:

"Because one beast *should* help another."

At this, Lordly Cock crowed with laughter, and picked up the seed in his beak, and carried it to the ant-hill for Lowly Ant. And when she thanked him, he gave her a proud and mighty bow, then went on strutting about the farmyard in his fine feather trousers.

Now just outside the farmyard gate, Wily Fox lay hidden in the long grass, watching Lordly Cock. And presently Lordly Cock heard a coaxing voice murmuring out of nowhere:

"Won't you crow us the time of day, mighty hero? Perhaps from the farmyard gate, where we can all admire you?"

At this, Lordly Cock felt *very* proud and mighty; and he flew up on to the farmyard gate, and flapped his wings, and lifted up his voice in a proud and mighty:

"Cock-a-doodle-doo!"

Then the coaxing voice murmured again out of nowhere:

"Beau-ti-ful! But didn't you know, mighty hero, that the proudest and most mighty heroes crow with their eyes shut?"

So Lordly Cock flapped his wings and closed his eyes and lifted up his voice again in an even prouder and mightier:

"Cock-a-doodle-doo!"

And while his eyes were closed, Wily Fox pounced on him, tearing his fine feather trousers; and with Lordly

Cock held fast between his teeth, away he went like the wind towards his distant den.

Now from her ant-hill Lowly Ant had seen this happen. So now she went toiling as quickly as she could to Lordly Cock's Favourite Hen, and told her:

"Favourite Hen, Wily Fox has caught our Lordly Cock, our proud and mighty hero, and torn his feather trousers, and carried him off to eat him!"

Then Favourite Hen called out to Duck:

"Duck, Lowly Ant says Wily Fox has caught our Lordly Cock, our proud and mighty hero, and torn his feather trousers, and carried him off to eat him!"

Then Duck called out to Goose:

"Goose, Favourite Hen says Lowly Ant says Wily Fox has caught our Lordly Cock, our proud and mighty hero, and torn his feather trousers, and carried him off to eat him!"

Then Goose called out to Dog:

"Dog, Duck says Favourite Hen says Lowly Ant says Wily Fox has caught our Lordly Cock, our proud and mighty hero, and torn his feather trousers, and carried him off to eat him!"

Then Dog called out to Sheep:

"Sheep, Goose says Duck says Favourite Hen says Lowly Ant says Wily Fox has caught our Lordly Cock, our proud and mighty hero, and torn his feather trousers, and carried him off to eat him!"

Then Sheep called out to Horse:

"Horse, Dog says Goose says Duck says Favourite Hen says Lowly Ant says Wily Fox has caught our Lordly Cock, our proud and mighty hero, and torn his feather trousers, and carried him off to eat him!"

Then Horse called out to Cow:

"Cow, Sheep says Dog says Goose says Duck says Favourite Hen says Lowly Ant says Wily Fox has caught our Lordly Cock, our proud and mighty hero, and torn his feather trousers, and carried him off to eat him!"

Then Cow called out to Milk-maid:

"Milk-maid, Horse says Sheep says Dog says Goose says Duck says Favourite Hen says Lowly Ant says Wily Fox has caught our Lordly Cock, our proud and mighty hero, and torn his feather trousers, and carried him off to eat him!"

Then Milk-maid called out to Farmer:

"Farmer, Cow says Horse says Sheep says Dog says Goose says Duck says Favourite Hen says Lowly Ant says Wily Fox has caught our Lordly Cock, our proud and mighty hero, and torn his feather trousers, and carried him off to eat him!"

And as soon as Farmer heard this, he opened the farmyard gate, and ran after Wily Fox; and Milk-maid ran after Farmer; and Cow ran after Milk-Maid; and Horse ran after Cow; and Sheep ran after Horse; and Dog ran after Sheep; and Goose ran after Dog; and Duck ran after Goose; and Favourite Hen ran after Duck; and Lowly Ant came toiling after them all.

And Farmer shouted; and Milk-maid screamed; and Cow mooed; and Horse neighed; and Sheep bleated; and Dog barked; and Goose cackled; and Duck quacked; and Favourite Hen clucked; and Lowly Ant was silent, for she needed all her breath to come toiling after them all.

Then Lordly Cock said to Wily Fox, as he hung between his jaws:

"You will never reach your den with me, Wily Fox! Can't you hear that Farmer and Milk-maid and Cow and Horse and Sheep and Dog and Goose and Duck and Favourite Hen are close behind, while Lowly Ant is toiling after them all?"

And Wily Fox replied:

"Bah! I can *easily* outrun Farmer, Milk-maid, Cow,

Horse, Sheep, Dog, Goose, Duck, Favourite Hen, *and* Lowly Ant who is toiling after them all!"

And while Wily Fox's mouth was open, saying this, Lordly Cock slipped from between his teeth, and flew into a tree, and flapped his wings, and lifted up his voice in the proudest and the mightiest and the most triumphant "Cock-a-doodle-doo!" you ever heard.

Then up came Farmer and Milk-maid and Cow and Horse and Sheep and Dog and Goose and Duck and Favourite Hen; and Lowly Ant came toiling after them all. And Wily Fox slunk home to his den empty-handed.

Then Lordly Cock flew down from the tree and bowed his thanks to Farmer. And Farmer said:

"Don't thank *me*, Lordly Cock. Thank Milk-maid. *She* told me."

Then Lordly Cock bowed his thanks to Milk-maid. But Milk-maid said:

"Don't thank *me*, Lordly Cock. Thank Cow. *She* told me."

Then Lordly Cock bowed his thanks to Cow. But Cow said:

"Don't thank *me*, Lordly Cock. Thank Horse. *He* told me."

Then Lordly Cock bowed his thanks to Horse. But Horse said:

"Don't thank *me*, Lordly Cock. Thank Sheep. *He* told me."

Then Lordly Cock bowed his thanks to Sheep. But Sheep said:

"Don't thank *me*, Lordly Cock. Thank Dog. *He* told me."

Then Lordly Cock bowed his thanks to Dog. But Dog said:

"Don't thank *me*, Lordly Cock. Thank Goose. *She* told me."

Then Lordly Cock bowed his thanks to Goose. But Goose said:

"Don't thank *me*, Lordly Cock. Thank Duck. *She* told me."

Then Lordly Cock bowed his thanks to Duck. But Duck said:

"Don't thank *me*, Lordly Cock. Thank Favourite Hen. *She* told me."

Then Lordly Cock bowed his thanks to Favourite Hen. But Favourite Hen said:

"Don't thank *me*, Lordly Cock. Thank Lowly Ant. *She* told me."

Then Lordly Cock bowed his thanks to Lowly Ant. And Lowly Ant waved her front legs politely, and said:

"Don't mention it, Lordly Cock. One beast *should* help another."

Then Favourite Hen said to Lordly Cock:

"And now, mighty hero, come home, my love, and let me mend those trousers!"

The Poem of Wily, Lordly and Lowly

That night Sylvia took all her farmyard animals — her cow and Brian and her sheep and Pip and her goose and her duck and her cock and her hen — to bed with her. She put her Wonder-Book on her bedside table, and she softly chanted her poetry spell:

"Rhyme-Elves, rich in ringing words
Won from winds and waves and birds,
Lisping leaves and rustling rain,
Sing — sing — for me again!"

And next morning, when she woke, she saw a new poem and a new picture on a new page. She looked first at the new picture, and chuckled over its portrait of Lordly Cock in his fine feather trousers. Then she took her Wonder-Book, and all her farmyard animals as well, into her mother's bed. And this was the new poem her mother read to them all:

Wily has a heart of stone.
He walks his woodland ways alone.
Alone he fares, alone he feasts:
He knows no brotherhood of beasts.
O Wily Fox!
If your cold heart should yearn to find
Kind fellowship, *you* must be kind,
Poor Wily!

Lordly is a sultan proud.
His comb glares red, and his voice crows loud.
He struts with pomp and glances grim.
His feather trousers flaunt on him.
O Lordly Cock!
Your bluff heart yet can learn that kings
Are kith and kin with creeping things,
Vain Lordly!

Lowly is small and black as soot,
And big beasts tread her underfoot;
Yet ever brave and brisk is she
To aid them in adversity.
O Lowly Ant!
As wakefully your ways you wend,
You are the whole world's tiny friend,
Dear Lowly!

Sylvia's Turnip-Lantern

On the last night of October there was to be a Hallowe'en Party in the village, and after dark all the children were to go in a procession with their lighted Hallowe'en lanterns hollowed out of turnips. So that morning, after Sylvia had helped her mother to sweep and dust, she asked:

"Shall I run into the garden now, Mother, and get a turnip for my lantern?"

And her mother said:

"Do you think you can pull it up all by yourself?"

And Sylvia answered:

"I'm sure I can!"

So Sylvia ran into the garden, and looked at all the turnips, and chose the one with the biggest leaves, and began to pull and pull. But the turnip tucked its head into the earth and did not move. So Sylvia took a deep breath and pulled again. But still the turnip did not move. Then she took a deeper breath, and pulled and pulled again. And suddenly she sat down backwards with a bang, with a big, white, chubby turnip in her hands.

And when she had taken it indoors and carefully washed it and dried it, her mother helped her to scoop it out inside, and then to carve a face outside, with a long, curved, smiling mouth. And then Sylvia put a candle inside, and lit it, and stood it in a dark cupboard, to see what it would look like at the party.

And the candle-light shone soft and rosy inside the turnip-head, turning it into a beautiful lantern. And inside her own head Sylvia saw a picture of all those rosy lanterns — hers and Joan's and Terry's and Rosaleen's and

Margaret's and Luke's and Stephen's — bobbing through the darkness along the village street.

And Sylvia said to her mother:

"The turnip looks so lovely now that it must be glad it let me pull it up; but at first it didn't want to come at all."

And her mother smiled and said:

"Perhaps you didn't pull it up in the right way."

Then Sylvia's eyes opened wide in surprise, and she asked:

"Why, Mother, is there a right way and a wrong way to pull up a turnip?"

And her mother answered:

"Hugin found there was when *he* tried to pull up *his* turnip."

And Sylvia exclaimed:

"Oh, Mother, is it a story? *Do* tell me!"

So while her mother scooped a little more here and there inside the turnip to make the lantern rosier yet, and made the smiling face outside the turnip still more smiling, she told Sylvia the Story of Hugin and the Turnip.

And this is it:

The Story of Hugin and the Turnip

Once upon a time there was a little boy named Hugin, and he wanted a turnip to make a Hallowe'en lantern, so he went out into the garden and planted a turnip-seed; and he said:

"Turnip, Turnip, grow for me;
Grow as big as big can be,
That I may make for Hallowe'en
The finest lantern ever seen.
I-want-to-put-a-candle-in-you, Turnip."

54

So the turnip grew as big as big could be, till it was so big that it *nearly* filled the garden.

Then Hugin went out to pull the turnip up. And he pulled and he pulled; but the turnip did not budge an inch.

Just then a lion came by, and asked:

"What are you doing, Hugin?"

And Hugin replied:

"I'm pulling up a turnip.

Lion, Lion, pull with me;
Pull as hard as hard can be,
That I may make for Hallowe'en
The finest lantern ever seen.
I-want-to-put-a-candle-in-my-turnip."

So Lion pulled Hugin, and Hugin pulled the turnip; they pulled and they pulled, but the turnip did not budge an inch.

Just then a bear came along, and asked:

"What are you doing, Lion?"

And Lion replied:

"I'm helping Hugin to pull up a turnip."

And Hugin said:

"Bear, Bear, pull with me;
Pull as hard as hard can be,
That I may make for Hallowe'en
The finest lantern ever seen.
I-want-to-put-a-candle-in-my-turnip."

So Bear pulled Lion, and Lion pulled Hugin, and Hugin pulled the turnip; they pulled and they pulled, but the turnip did not budge an inch.

Just then a fox came by, and asked:

"What are you doing, Bear?"

And Bear replied:

"I'm helping Lion to help Hugin to pull up a turnip."

And Hugin said:

"Fox, Fox, pull with me;
Pull as hard as hard can be,
That I may make for Hallowe'en
The finest lantern ever seen.
I-want-to-put-a-candle-in-my-turnip."

So Fox pulled Bear, and Bear pulled Lion, and Lion pulled Hugin, and Hugin pulled the turnip; they pulled and they pulled, but the turnip did not budge an inch.

Just then a hare came by, and asked:

"What are you doing, Fox?"

And Fox replied:

"I'm helping Bear to help Lion to help Hugin to pull up a turnip."

And Hugin said:

"Hare, Hare, pull with me;
Pull as hard as hard can be,
That I may make for Hallowe'en
The finest lantern ever seen.
I-want-to-put-a-candle-in-my-turnip."

So Hare pulled Fox, and Fox pulled Bear, and Bear pulled Lion, and Lion pulled Hugin, and Hugin pulled the turnip; they pulled and they pulled, but the turnip did not budge an inch.

Just then a mouse came by, and asked:

"What are you doing, Hare?"

And Hare replied:

"I'm helping Fox to help Bear to help Lion to help Hugin to pull up a turnip."

And Hugin said:

> "Mouse, Mouse, pull with me;
> Pull as hard as hard can be,
> That I may make for Hallowe'en
> The finest lantern ever seen.
> I-want-to-put-a-candle-in-my-turnip."

So Mouse pulled Hare, and Hare pulled Fox, and Fox pulled Bear, and Bear pulled Lion, and Lion pulled Hugin, and Hugin pulled the turnip; they pulled and they pulled, but the turnip did not budge an inch.

Just then a caterpillar came by, and asked:

"What are you doing, Mouse?"

And Mouse replied:

"I'm helping Hare to help Fox to help Bear to help Lion to help Hugin to pull up a turnip."

And Caterpillar said:

"But does Hugin know the right way to pull up a turnip? Did he first ask its root-gnome if he might?"

Then Hugin bent down and put his mouth close to the ground, and called:

> "Gnome, Gnome, good Root-Gnome,
> May I take your turnip home,
> That I may make for Hallowe'en
> The finest lantern ever seen?
> I-want-to-put-a-candle-in-your-turnip."

And at once a little root-gnome popped up his brown head out of the ground, and said:

"Good gracious me, Hugin, why didn't you *tell* me? All this time I've been pulling the other way, when there's nothing a root-gnome likes better than a candle put in his turnip! Now pull again!"

And he popped back his brown head into the ground.

So Caterpillar pulled Mouse, and Mouse pulled Hare, and Hare pulled Fox, and Fox pulled Bear, and Bear pulled Lion, and Lion pulled Hugin, and Hugin pulled the turnip. And suddenly Mouse sat down backwards with a bang on Caterpillar, and Hare sat down backwards with a bang on Mouse, and Fox sat down backwards with a bang on Hare, and Bear sat down backwards with a bang on Fox, and Lion sat down backwards with a bang on Bear, and Hugin sat down backwards with a bang on Lion, with the biggest, whitest, chubbiest turnip in his hand that ever anyone saw!

Then Hugin got up and said "Sorry" to Lion; and Lion got up and said "Sorry" to Bear; and Bear got up and said "Sorry" to Fox; and Fox got up and said "Sorry" to Hare; and Hare got up and said "Sorry" to Mouse; and Mouse got up and said "Sorry" to Caterpillar. And nobody was hurt, and everybody laughed, and Hugin put-a-candle-in-his-turnip.

The Poem of Hallowe'en Lanterns

The Hallowe'en party was just as exciting as Sylvia had hoped, and the line of rosy lanterns along the dark village street was even more beautiful than Sylvia had pictured it would be.

When the party was over, the Old Woodsman came with Blackbird to bring Sylvia home; and she was so happily tired that on the way she fell asleep with her face buried in the tickling hairs of his old coat. She woke up just enough to get undressed; and when her mother had tucked her up in bed, she was only just able to put out her Wonder-Book beside her turnip-lantern on the bedside table, and to chant her poetry spell very drowsily —

> "Rhyme-Elves rich in ringing words
> Won from winds and waves and birds,
> Lisping leaves and rustling rain,
> Sing — sing — for me again!" —

before she fell sound asleep again.

And next morning, when she woke, quite fresh again, her Wonder-Book was open at a new page, and there was a new picture of Hugin and Lion and Bear and Fox and Hare and Mouse and Caterpillar pulling up the big turnip; and she sat up in bed and bubbled with laughter over it. And when she took the Wonder-Book into her mother's bed, this was the new poem her mother read to her:

> Beautiful are forests when the leaves are green;
> Beautiful are rainbows where a storm has been;
> Beautiful are lanterns in the night at Hallowe'en.
>
> Beautiful are lanterns gilding spring's gay shoots;
> Beautiful are lanterns firing autumn's fruits;
> Beautiful are lanterns carved from winter's earthy
>   roots.
>
> Hallowe'en lanterns swinging soft and slow;
> Hallowe'en lanterns filled with candle-glow —
> Gently shining candles, cupped in caves of rosy snow.
>
> Vegetable faces in a flickering file
> Shimmer on the darkness, sway and pause awhile,
> On each brow a brightness, and a star behind each
>   smile.

Sylvia and the Black Imp

One grey November afternoon, Sylvia was swinging on the garden gate while she watched for her mother to come back from the village, when suddenly a bouncing little voice called out:

"Hullo, Sylvia!"

And there, peeping from behind a tree-trunk in the dark wood, she saw a little black imp.

Sylvia said in surprise:

"Can you really see me? The earth-knights can't till I'm seven."

The black imp cut a caper, and snapped his little black fingers, and said disdainfully:

"They're only *ordinary* fairies. I can do *lots* of things they can't."

Sylvia was very much impressed by this, and said respectfully:

"Can you really? Do come into the garden and show me some."

But the black imp shuddered, and said:

"Not I. I just can't bear being inside a nut-hedge."

Now that ought to have warned Sylvia that the black imp was not the sort of fairy she ought to know, for the Old Woodsman had told her that the reason wise people had planted the nut-hedge round the garden was to keep bad goblins out. And what the black imp said next ought also to have warned her, for this is what it was:

"Why don't you come into the dark wood instead?"

And Sylvia told him:

"I'm not allowed to go there alone."

Then the black imp coaxed her:

"But you wouldn't be alone. You'd be with me."

Now Sylvia had not wanted at all to go into the dark wood without her mother until the black imp put the thought into her mind. But now she very much wanted to go, so she said hopefully:

"Perhaps Mother wouldn't so much mind my coming without her if Sister-in-the-Bushes came instead."

But the black imp made an ugly face, and said pettishly:

"Oh no — don't let's ask *her*. It would be much more fun just us two by ourselves. I know a secret place where you can find the most gorgeous spotted toadstools."

Sylvia asked:

"Could I bring some home for my mother?"

And the black imp answered:

"Of course you could — as many as ever you like."

Somehow that seemed to Sylvia to make it not quite so naughty; so she opened the gate, and out into the dark wood she went, with the black imp skipping in front and capering with glee.

And at first he made it a really fine adventure. He took Sylvia to a part of the dark wood she had never seen before, where yellow and scarlet and purple-spotted toadstools grew at the foot of the pines; and he showed her how to plant them in damp moss to make a little garden. And Sylvia picked them till both her pockets were quite full.

Then she began to have a feeling inside that it would soon be tea-time; so she said politely:

"Thank you *very* much, Black Imp. It's time I went home now."

But the black imp said:

"Oh, don't go yet, Sylvia. There's lots more to do and see. Let's go along *this* path."

And Sylvia was just about to follow him when a soft voice whispered in her ear:

"Don't go, Sylvia. That's the path to the bog."

Sylvia could see nobody there, but she knew the voice; it belonged to Sister-in-the Bushes. So she called:

"Oh no, Black Imp. I'm too tired."

So the black imp turned back, and suggested:

"Then let's sit down a bit on this soft moss."

Sylvia was very glad to sit down, for she suddenly did feel very weak and tired; but also she began to feel more and more certainly that it was tea-time; and presently she exclaimed:

"Oh dear, I *am* so hungry!"

And the black imp said:

"Then why not eat a nice toadstool? They're really very tasty. Look — have this one!"

And he picked a brilliant scarlet one growing close beside him.

And Sylvia was so hungry that she took it and was just going to bite it when Sister-in-the-Bushes' soft voice whispered again in her ear:

"Don't eat it, Sylvia. It's poisonous."

So Sylvia said:

"No, thank you, Black Imp. I'd like to go home now, please."

Then the black imp looked at her, and grinned wickedly, and said:

"But do you know your way? I don't. Look at all these paths — don't they all look like the same path?"

And that was quite true; yet all the same, Sylvia had a feeling that the black imp was mocking her. And she began to cry; for by now dusk was creeping through the dark wood, and she was frightened when she thought that she might still be lost in the woods when the cold, black night came on.

Then the black imp suggested:

"Why not come home with *me*?"

And Sylvia was so anxious not to be out in the dark

wood all night that she was just scrambling up to follow when the soft voice whispered again:

"Don't go home with the black imp, Sylvia. He lives in a deep, dark pool. But have a brave heart. Your mother will soon be here."

Then Sylvia looked round again; and this time she felt sure she saw the faint white figure of Sister-in-the-Bushes flitting away between the tree-trunks. So she dried her eyes; and no matter what pleasant thing the black imp suggested, she refused to move, though the evening shadows grew thicker all the time.

Then, far away, she heard her mother's voice calling faintly:

"Sylvia! Sylvia!"

And Sylvia jumped up and called back:

"Here, Mother! Oh, Mother, Mother, Mother!"

And then she saw again the faint white figure of Sister-in-the-Bushes, but this time flitting towards her; and following her, a lighted lantern flickered in and out among the trees; and she ran as fast as she could towards them, and threw herself, sobbing, sobbing, sobbing, into her mother's arms.

And her mother kissed her and comforted her, and all the way home she did not say a single cross word.

When they reached their white cottage, Sylvia felt so very tired that her mother said she should have a great treat — she should have tea in bed. And when Sylvia was undressed and sitting up in bed, with Kate, the elderly baby, comforting one side of her, and Titania, the fairy doll, comforting the other, and a hot-water bottle comforting her cold toes, her mother came in with warm milk and hot buttered toast; and Sylvia threw her arms round her and cried:

"Oh, Mother, I do love you so!"

And Sylvia's mother stroked her tangled curls back from

her forehead, and said: "Whatever a black imp wants you to do again, Sylvia, don't do it if he doesn't want Sister-in-the-Bushes to do it, too."

And Sylvia opened her eyes wide in surprise, and asked: "*How* did you know about the black imp, Mother?"

And her mother answered:

"Whenever anyone is disobedient, it is always because they have let a black imp persuade them. That was how the Youngest Prince came to grow that ugly long nose."

And Sylvia begged, already feeling much, much better at the prospect of a story:

"Oh, Mother, do tell me about him!"

So when Sylvia had finished her warm milk and her hot buttered toast, and had snuggled down into bed between Kate and Titania and the hot-water bottle, her mother sat on the edge of the bed and told them the Story of the Country at the Bottom of the Well.

And here it is:

The Story of the Country at the Bottom of the Well

The King of the shining Land of the Sun had three sons. Two of them worked hard, learning how to become kings themselves. But the Youngest Prince said to his father:

"Father, I do not want to learn how to become a king. I only want to wander about the kingdom, seeing new sights and people."

And the King replied:

"My son, you shall be free to wander for a year and a day. At the end of that time, return to the palace, and we will speak further on these matters."

And he gave the Youngest Prince five animals to be his friends and companions on his wanderings — an elephant, a giraffe, a stork, a monkey and a stoat. And the King said to the five animals:

"Whatever the Youngest Prince does, you must do. And wherever the Youngest Prince goes, you must go."

And to the Youngest Prince he gave this warning:

"Everything in the shining Land of the Sun is beautiful, and everything there except one thing is good. That is the silver cherry-tree. If you should come upon it, beware that you do not pick and eat any of its cherries, or they will lead you to disaster."

Then the Youngest Prince set out with his friends, the five animals. And each new thing he saw in the shining Land of the Sun was more beautiful than the last, until, in a hidden valley far away from anywhere, he came upon the silver cherry-tree, laden with glittering silver cherries. And he thought that this was the most beautiful thing of all.

When the Youngest Prince and the five animals came close to the silver cherry-tree, to admire it, they found that at its roots there was a well. And as they leaned over it and gazed down into its dark depths, the Youngest Prince remarked:

"I can see no water. I wonder what is at the bottom?"

And at once a voice replied, a hollow voice from a long, long distance down:

"My kingdom lies at the bottom of the well."

And the Youngest Prince exclaimed in surprise:

"How I should love to see a country at the bottom of a well!"

And the hollow voice replied:

"That is quite easy. All you have to do is to eat a silver cherry."

Then the Youngest Prince sighed and said:

"But the King my father has forbidden me to do that."

And the hollow voice replied:

"There is no other way."

Now the Youngest Prince longed to see the Country at the Bottom of the Well, for he loved seeing all new things. So he pushed away the memory of his father's warning, and he said to the five animals:

"I am going to eat a silver cherry. Will you eat one with me?"

And the elephant and the giraffe and the stork and the monkey and the stoat answered together:

"Whatever the Youngest Prince does, we will do. Wherever the Youngest Prince goes, we will go."

So the Youngest Prince reached up to the silver cherry-tree, and he picked a bunch of six silver cherries, and he gave one to each of the animals, and kept one for himself. And each ate his silver cherry, and the six cherry-stones they placed in a ring at the foot of the tree.

And at once a wind arose, and caught them up, and whirled them — prince, elephant, giraffe, stork, monkey, stoat — down, down, down into the darkness, and set them on their feet in the Country at the Bottom of the Well.

After the brightness and the beauty of the shining Land of the Sun, the Country at the Bottom of the Well seemed to them dark and wild and ugly. The light was grey, for here there shone no sun; there were no flowers, but everywhere there were marshes and old mine-shafts and gaunt cliffs and chasms.

And as the Youngest Prince and the five animals looked about them in dismay, they heard mocking laughter behind them; and turning, they saw the King of that country coming towards them in a crown of lead, his courtiers close behind him. And the King was a black imp. And all his courtiers were black imps, too.

And the King of the Black Imps shouted:

"Welcome, Prince Long-Nose!"

And all the black imps laughed mockingly.

Then the King of the Black Imps shouted again:

"Welcome, Elephant Finger-Face, Giraffe Head-in-Air, Stork Spindle-Shanks, Monkey Flapping-Sleeves, Stoat Snake-Body!"

And all the black imps laughed mockingly again.

Now every person and every animal in the shining Land of the Sun was beautiful. So now the Youngest Prince and the five animals looked in surprise at one another, wondering what the King of the Black Imps could mean.

And they found that it was quite true. The beautiful young prince had grown a long, long nose; the elephant had grown a long finger on his face; the giraffe's neck had shot up until his head was lifted far away; the stork's legs had lengthened into two tall, bony stilts; the monkey's arms hung to the ground like sleeves that needed shortening; and the stoat's body had stretched lengthways till he did look rather like a snake on legs.

And the Youngest Prince and the five animals all began to ache all over with their new ugliness.

Then the Youngest Prince cried in dismay:

"What can have made us all so ugly — so ugly that we ache all over with it?"

And the King of the Black Imps answered gloatingly:

"Eating the silver cherries has done that."

Then the Youngest Prince said haughtily:

"I have seen enough of this Country at the Bottom of the Well. I wish to return now to the shining Land of the Sun."

But the King of the Black Imps again laughed mockingly, and told him:

"You will never see the sun again, Prince Long-Nose. For the only way to climb to the top of the well is by a secret stair; and to that secret stair nothing except the golden pear can lead you. But the golden pear is so cunningly hidden that you could never find it; and even if you did, my black imps would steal it from you."

So now all Prince Long-Nose longed for was to find the golden pear; and he and the five animals began to wander all over the Country at the Bottom of the Well in search of it. They wandered through marshy regions, and they wandered through regions of old mine-shafts, and they wandered through regions of cliffs and chasms; but nowhere could they find the golden pear.

Now the prince's ugly long nose was aware of scents which his beautiful short one would never have noticed. And one day, as he and the five animals were passing the mouth of a small cave, his long nose twitched, and he paused and twitched it again, then cried in excitement:

"I can smell pears!"

So, following the pear-scent, he led the five animals into the cave and further and further in along a narrow rocky passage. And after a while they saw ahead of them light brighter than any light they had yet seen in this dark country. And when they reached the end of the passage, they stepped out into a desolate plain, on which nothing grew except one solitary tree in the middle. And the gleaming of this tree lit up all that desolate plain.

Then Prince Long-Nose and the five animals rushed across that desolate plain to this gleaming tree. And they found it was indeed the golden pear-tree, for on it hung one solitary gleaming, golden pear.

Then, with thankfulness and joy, Prince Long-Nose picked the golden pear. And it slipped through his fingers to the ground, and began to move as if drawn by an unseen thread, leading them back by the shortest way to the bottom of the well.

Over rough hills they followed it, till they came into a region of old mine-shafts. And suddenly, out of nowhere, a black imp pounced upon the golden pear, and darted with it to the nearest mine-shaft, and flung it into it with all his might. Then Prince Long-Nose stopped short in dismay; and so did Elephant Finger-Face, Giraffe Head-in-Air, Stork Spindle-Shanks, and Monkey Flapping-Sleeves.

But Stoat Snake-Body bowed and said:

"By your leave, Youngest Prince!"

And into the mine-shaft he went, his long body burrowing; and the others held their breath as they waited. And presently out he came again, and in his mouth was the golden pear.

Then again the golden pear slipped to the ground and began to move as if drawn by an unseen thread, leading them back by the shortest way to the bottom of the well.

Through thorny thickets they followed it, till they came into a region of narrow passes winding between steep chasms. And suddenly, out of nowhere, a second black imp pounced upon the golden pear, and darted with it to the nearest chasm, and flung it over with all his might. And when the prince and the animals looked over the edge, they could see the golden pear gleaming far, far below like a fallen star. Then Prince Long-Nose stared down at it in dismay; and so did Elephant Finger-Face, Giraffe Head-in-Air, Stork Spindle-Shanks and Stoat Snake-Body.

But Monkey Flapping-Sleeves bowed and said:

"By your leave, Youngest Prince!"

And over the edge he went, and down the steep face of the precipice, clinging with his long arms to every piece of jutting rock and every trailing creeper; and the others held their breath as they waited. And presently up and over the edge he came again, and in his mouth was the golden pear.

Then again the golden pear slipped to the ground, and began to move as if drawn by an unseen thread, leading them back by the shortest way to the bottom of the well.

Across bleak moors they followed it, till they came into a region of treacherous marshes. And suddenly, out of nowhere, a third black imp pounced upon the golden pear, and darted with it to the brink of the nearest marsh, and flung it into it with all his might. And the deep mud closed right over the golden pear, leaving nothing to mark the spot where it had disappeared.

Then Prince Long-Nose stared at the marsh in dismay; and so did Elephant Finger-Face, Giraffe Head-in-Air, Monkey Flapping-Sleeves and Stoat Snake-Body.

But Stork Spindle-Shanks bowed and said:

"By your leave, Youngest Prince!"

And into the marsh he waded, his long, bony stilts of legs carrying him safely through the deep mud, which his long beak stabbed here, there, and everywhere; and the others held their breath as they waited. And presently back he came, and in his beak was the golden pear.

Then again the golden pear slipped to the ground, and began to move as if drawn by an unseen thread, leading them back by the shortest way to the bottom of the well.

Between barren mountains they followed it, till they came to a region of tall cliffs and deep gorges. And suddenly, out of nowhere, a fourth black imp pounced upon the golden pear and darted with it up the face of the nearest tall cliff, and tossed it into the nest of a bird of prey on one of the cliff's high ledges. The fledglings in the nest began to scream, and the angry parent birds came circling threateningly round the prince and his animals below, ready to attack if they tried to climb the cliff. And Prince Long-Nose stared at them in dismay; and so did Elephant Finger-Face, Stork Spindle-Shanks, Monkey Flapping-Sleeves and Stoat Snake-Body.

But Giraffe Head-in-Air bowed and said:

"By your leave, Youngest Prince!"

And high above the circling birds of prey he lifted his long neck, and into the nest and between the screaming fledglings he darted his head; and the others held their breath as they waited. And presently he bent his long neck again, and between his lips was the golden pear.

Then again the golden pear slipped to the ground, and began to move as if drawn by an unseen thread, leading them back by the shortest way to the bottom of the well.

Across a dreary desert they followed it; and already they were within sight of the bottom of the well when suddenly, out of nowhere, a fifth black imp pounced upon the golden pear, and darted with it into a crevice between rocks which was far to small for anyone but a black imp to enter.

Then Prince Long-Nose stared at the crevice in dismay; and so did Giraffe Head-in-Air, Stork Spindle-Shanks, Monkey Flapping-Sleeves and Stoat Snake-Body.

But Elephant Finger-Face bowed and said:

"By your leave, Youngest Prince!"

And he marched forward, trumpeting loudly, and brandished his long trunk; and with it he tore rock from rock, and with it he searched beyond them; and the others held their breath as they waited. And presently back he came, and tucked safely into the end of his trunk was the golden pear.

Then again the golden pear slipped to the ground, and began to move as if drawn by an unseen thread. And it moved to the bottom of the well; and the rock parted before it, revealing a secret stair inside the wall of the well. And the golden pear began to move up the secret stair; and Prince Long-Nose and Elephant Finger-Face and Giraffe Head-in-Air and Stork Spindle-Shanks and Monkey Flapping-Sleeves and Stoat Snake-Body followed it. And the rock closed again behind them, shutting the black imps out.

And at the top of the well they came out into the warmth and the golden light and the green grass and the beauty of the shining Land of the Sun. And there, under the silver cherry-tree, stood the prince's father in his golden crown and his royal robes, gazing sadly at the ring of six cherry-stones. For the year and a day set for the prince's wanderings were long over; and the King had been searching throughout his kingdom for him; and when he had found the six cherry-stones under the silver cherry-tree, he had feared that his youngest son was lost to him for ever.

So now he took Prince Long-Nose joyfully in his arms; and when he saw the prince's long nose, and the elephant's long trunk, and the giraffe's long neck, and the stork's long legs, and the monkey's long arms, and the stoat's long body, he set the golden pear upright in the middle of the ring of cherry-stones; and the golden pear fell into six pieces as cleanly as if you had cut it with a knife; and each piece lay over a cherry-stone.

And to Prince Long-Nose and to each of the five animals the King gave a piece of the golden pear to eat. And after they had eaten it they were no longer Prince Long-Nose and Elephant Finger-Face and Giraffe Head-in-Air and Stork Spindle-Shanks and Monkey Flapping-Sleeves and Stoat Snake-Body, but they once more became as beautiful as they had been before they ate the silver cherries. And in the same moment they all ceased to ache all over.

And the Youngest Prince exclaimed:

"Father, I am cured of wandering. Let me start at once learning how to be a king!"

Then they all went back to the palace, where a rich banquet was prepared for them. And the King and the three young princes and the five beautiful animals all sat down to the banquet, and in great joy feasted together.

The Poem of the Silver Cherry and the Golden Pear

When Sylvia's mother had finished the story, Sylvia felt so sleepy that, although it was only just after tea-time, she at once put out her Wonder-Book and softly chanted her poetry spell:

> "Rhyme-Elves, rich in ringing words
> Won from winds and waves and birds,
> Lisping leaves and rustling rain,
> Sing — sing — for me again!"

And no sooner had her mother tucked Sylvia and Kate and Titania and the hot-water bottle in cosily, and taken the tea-tray, and turned out the light, than Sylvia went as fast asleep as if it were really bed-time.

And she slept so soundly, in spite of her adventure with the black imp, that when she woke it was morning, and she felt quite fresh again. And there, on a new page of the Wonder-Book, was a happy picture of the Youngest Prince and the five animals, finding the golden pear-tree. And when Sylvia and Kate and Titania took the Wonder-Book into Sylvia's mother's bed, this was the new poem she read out to them:

> O Youngest Prince!
> This silver cherry in your hand
> Will lay on you a hideous spell,
> And drive you from the sun, to dwell
> In the wild, ugly, sunless land
> At the black bottom of the well.

O Youngest Prince!
Follow the gracious golden pear
That lights up all this desolate plain;
And it shall heal you of your pain,
And lead you up the secret stair
Back to your shining home again.

Sylvia's Advent Wreath

One frosty morning right at the end of November, Sylvia's mother said:

"Only a month now till Christmas, Sylvia! Shall we go into the wood today, and get the pine-boughs for our Advent wreath?"

So out along the woodland path they went. Sylvia had thought at first, after her adventure with the black imp, that she would never love the dark wood again; but she found she loved it just as much as ever, and today she did not even think of the black imp once.

Sylvia and her mother came home laden with pine-boughs, which they twisted round a hoop of wire to make a thick green wreath. Then they fastened four tall white candles to the wreath, and with a long loop of broad red ribbon they hung it from the ceiling of the cottage living-room.

And when it was dark and the curtains were drawn, Sylvia's mother lifted Sylvia to the green wreath with a lighted taper, so that she could light the first candle. Next week there would be two candles lit every evening, and the next week three, till each evening of the last week before Christmas all four would be softly shining.

Sylvia sat on the hearth in front of the blazing log fire, and leaned back happily against her mother's knee, and looked up at the gentle candle-glow falling on the red ribbon and the dark green wreath; and she said:

"It's like an evergreen crown, isn't it, Mother, with a jewel in the candle-flame?"

And her mother replied:

"That's why Rufusi Ryneker so much longed to wear it."

And Sylvia exclaimed:

"Rufusi Ryneker? What a fine name! Who was he, Mother?"

So, sitting quietly in the firelight and the candle-light, Sylvia's mother told her the Story of Rufusi Ryneker.

And this is the story:

The Story of Rufusi Ryneker

There was once a fox with a fine red coat. His name was Rufusi Ryneker, a fine name for a fox. But the finest thing about him was his fine red brush.

Rufusi Ryneker's fine red brush was very clever. When Rufusi Ryneker was being hunted, his fine red brush helped him to escape, for it stretched out behind him and balanced his long body, so that he could swiftly swerve and change his direction, leaving the hounds and the huntsmen far behind.

And when it was Rufusi Ryneker himself who was hunting, again it was his fine red brush that helped him. For Rufusi Ryneker would lie hidden in the long grasses, and his fine red brush would wave about with the tip just showing; and all the little curious birds, and especially the larks, would come flying close to discover what this waving red plume was; and in this way the fine red brush brought Rufusi Ryneker many a toothsome dinner.

One day when Rufusi Ryneker was lying hidden in the grass and his fine red brush was catching larks for his dinner, Rufusi Ryneker heard the blowing of the hunting-horns and the shouts of the huntsmen and the baying of the hounds; and up and away he went like a streak of glossy red lightning.

He twisted and turned across the countryside, his fine

red brush helping him, till he came to a river, and swam across to the other side. It was a very muddy river, and he came ashore in a very muddy place.

Presently the blowing of the horns and the shouts of the huntsmen and the baying of the hounds told him that they, too, had crossed the river. So Rufusi Ryneker began to run once more. But now he found that his fine red brush was heavy with water and mud, so that instead of stretching out behind and helping him, it kept dragging on the ground.

Rufusi Ryneker came to a forest, and entered it, hoping he might escape by twisting and turning among the trees; but the shouting huntsmen and the baying hounds were now so near that he knew they must soon overtake him. And then, just as he lost heart, a little house with a green door rose up suddenly out of the forest path in front of him; and a little man stood holding the green door open; and the little man beckoned, and called:

"Rufusi Ryneker! Come in quickly!"

Rufusi Ryneker darted in at the open green door, and the little man snapped it shut, and stamped three times, and chanted:

"Down, little house,
Below the ground!
Down, little house;
Be no more found!"

And immediately the little house sank down right into the earth, and the forest path closed over its roof as if it were not there.

When Rufusi Ryneker had recovered his breath, he began to look round the little house, and he saw that hanging by red ribbons from the painted ceiling was a crown of pine-boughs, and on the crown of pine-boughs were four lighted white candles with pure golden flames, and at the heart of each golden flame there shone a jewel.

And Rufusi Ryneker looked at the crown of pine-boughs with joy, and with joy, and with great joy.

And he asked:

"Whose is this crown of candles, and why does it hang here?"

And the little man replied:

"It comes down from the skies, and it hangs here because this is the House of Crowning. I am All-Wise the Dwarf, and every winter I search among all the creatures in the forest, and when I have found the wisest, I crown him with this crown; and if he really is the wisest, then the gems in the flames of the candles will light up his head."

Then Rufusi Ryneker looked again at the crown with joy, and with joy, and with great joy; and he longed above all things to be crowned with it.

And he said:

"Oh, All-Wise, *I* am wise. I am sure I must be the wisest of all the creatures in the forest!"

Then All-Wise the Dwarf looked at Rufusi Ryneker; and he answered:

"You are very, very *clever*, Rufusi Ryneker; but are you really *wise*? For instance, do you know whose fault it was that the hounds almost caught you today?"

Then Rufusi Ryneker asked his four feet:

"Four Feet, my servants, was it *your* fault that the hounds almost caught me today?"

And Rufusi Ryneker's four feet answered:

"No, Rufusi Ryneker. We carried you swiftly and surely, as we always do."

Then Rufusi Ryneker asked his two eyes:

"Two Eyes, my servants, was it *your* fault that the hounds almost caught me today?"

And Rufusi Ryneker's two eyes answered:

"No, Rufusi Ryneker. We were very watchful, as we always are."

Then Rufusi Ryneker asked his two ears:

"Two Ears, my servants, was it *your* fault that the hounds almost caught me today?"

And Rufusi Ryneker's two ears answered:

"No, Rufusi Ryneker. As always, we were wide open and listening hard."

Then Rufusi Ryneker asked his fine red brush:

"Red Brush, my servant, was it *your* fault that the hounds almost caught me today?"

And Rufusi Ryneker's fine red brush answered:

"Yes, Rufusi Ryneker. I dragged on the ground."

Then Rufusi Ryneker was furious with his fine red brush, and he cried to All-Wise the Dwarf:

"Give me your knife, All-Wise! I shall cut off Red Brush, my servant, and throw him away."

But All-Wise replied:

"First let Red Brush tell us *why* he dragged on the ground."

And the fine red brush explained:

"Because I was heavy with water and mud from the river."

Then All-Wise the Dwarf asked further:

"And why were you heavy, Red Brush?"

And the fine red brush answered:

"Because Rufusi Ryneker did not shake me enough when he came out of the river, and came ashore in a very muddy place."

Then All-Wise the Dwarf said:

"Think again, Rufusi Ryneker. Whose fault was it *really* that the hounds almost caught you today?"

And Rufusi Ryneker confessed humbly:

"It was not Red Brush my servant's fault; it was my own. You are right, All-Wise; I am not wise, but only clever. How did you know? And how can I learn to be wise?"

And All-Wise the Dwarf replied:

"I knew because you did not say 'Thank you' when you came in at my green door. Learn to be grateful, Rufusi Ryneker, to your servants who serve you so faithfully, and to the stones on which you tread, and to the plants which shelter you, and to the air you breathe, and to the sun which gives you light. That is how you will grow wise. And one day you will come again on some forest path to the little House of Crowning, and I will hold its green door open, and I will say, 'Come in, Rufusi Ryneker,' and I will crown you with the crown of candles, and the gems in the hearts of their flames will light up your head."

Then All-Wise the Dwarf stamped three times, and said to the House of Crowning:

"Up, little house,
To sun and air!
Up, little house,
To the forest fair!"

And immediately the House of Crowning rose above the ground, and All-Wise the Dwarf opened the little green door, and Rufusi Ryneker saw that they were in the middle of the forest path again, and the hounds and the huntsmen had gone, and night had fallen, and the stars were shining.

And as Rufusi Ryneker said thank you and farewell to All-Wise the Dwarf and made his way home through the night, he began to feel quite differently towards Four Feet, and Two Eyes, and Two Ears, and Red Brush, who served him so quietly and faithfully, and to the trees which sheltered him, and to the stars which lit the darkness, and to the stones which made earth firm beneath his feet.

81

And at the memory of the crown of candles hanging in the little House of Crowning, and at the hope that All-Wise would one day crown him with it and that the gems at the hearts of the flames of the candles would light up his head, Rufusi Ryneker's heart was filled with joy, and with joy, and with great joy.

The Poem of the Crown of Candles

When the story was finished, Sylvia helped her mother to prepare the Advent apples. They chose the four rosiest, and scooped out the core; and in each apple, in the hole where the core had been, they set a coloured candle. And when supper-time came, they put an Advent apple at each corner of the table, and lit the coloured candles, and had their meal by candlelight. And as the gentle glow and the gentle shadows fell on the Christmas roses in the middle of the table, and on the bowl of apples and oranges, and on Sylvia's mother's face, Sylvia thought they made everything lovelier.

Sylvia took one of the candles in its apple candlestick with her when she went to bed, and it turned the open page of her Wonder-Book golden as she softly chanted her poetry spell:

> "Rhyme-Elves, rich in ringing words
> Won from winds and waves and birds,
> Lisping leaves and rustling rain,
> Sing — sing — for me again!"

And next morning, on the new page, there was a fine portrait of Rufusi Ryneker and his fine red brush to be enjoyed; and when she took the Wonder-Book into her

mother's bed, this was the new poem her mother read to
her:

> Rufusi, Rufusi Ryneker,
> Clever you are!
> But when have you paused to be grateful
> To stone or to star;
> To air or to sun or to water,
> To scent or to snow,
> To all things and creatures that save you and serve
>   you,
> Above and below?
>
> Rufusi, Rufusi Ryneker,
> Thus will you grow wise;
> And then will you find in the forest
> The crown of the skies;
> And when to the House of your Crowning
> You one day are led,
> The gems at the hearts of the flames of the candles
> Shall light up your head.

The Visit of St Nicholas

A few days later, Sylvia had a St Nicholas Eve party; and to it she invited her six little friends — Joan and Terry and Rosaleen and Margaret and Stephen and Luke.

The Old Woodsman had said to Sylvia that morning:

"You know, tonight's the night when St Nicholas goes about the world, visiting little children. I wonder whether he will visit *you*?"

And Sylvia told Joan and Terry and Rosaleen and Margaret and Stephen and Luke; so when, in the middle of "Hunt the slipper," there suddenly came three loud knocks at the door, they all became as still as mice, and everyone was thinking:

"I wonder if that's St Nicholas?"

Then Sylvia's mother said quietly:

"Open the door, Sylvia, and see who is there!"

So Sylvia got up and went to the door; and her heart was going *thump — thump — thump*. And she opened the door; and there stood St Nicholas.

And St Nicholas asked:

"May I come in, Sylvia?"

And Sylvia opened the door wider, and St Nicholas came in, in a magnificent red cloak, with his golden bishop's mitre on his head, and with his golden bishop's crook in his hand, and under his arm an enormous golden book.

And behind him came capering his little black page-boy, Rupert, with a stick in one hand, and a birch-twig broom in the other, and a bulging sack over one shoulder, and a twinkle in both eyes.

And all the children still sat like mice in their circle on the carpet, and stared and stared and stared. But Sylvia's mother welcomed St Nicholas, and offered him a chair; and St Nicholas thanked her and sat down, with Rupert standing beside him.

Then St Nicholas looked round at all the children, and said:

"In this big golden book of mine are the names of all the children everywhere in the world; and their good deeds are written on the golden pages, and their bad deeds on the black ones."

And he opened the book at a black page. Yet nobody felt hurt or scolded when he read out their faults; for always, with a hop, skip and a jump and with a twinkle in both eyes, the little black page-boy Rupert landed in front of each child, and out of his bulging sack came some lovely gift to help to overcome each fault. Sylvia's was a box of the most beautiful velvet hair-ribbons she had ever seen, to help her to stop getting her curls all over tangles; and it was just as if Rupert had been peeping into her wardrobe, for there was a velvet ribbon to match every dress she had.

And all the time Rupert cut so many capers and was so full of fun and antics that soon the children were all rolling about with laughter.

Then St Nicholas turned to a golden page, and told Rupert to reward the children for what it said about them there; so open came Rupert's sack again, and out came the loveliest gifts, just the very things each child most longed for. And to Sylvia, Rupert gave a set of little biscuit-cutters shaped like stars and hearts and crescent moons and flowers and tiny trees — exactly what she wanted for cutting out biscuits for Christmas and her birthday.

Then Rupert chased all the children with his big stick, and the shrieks of merriment grew louder and louder. And he lent the children his birch-twig broom to take turns in sweeping up the silver paper and coloured wools and other things from the party till the room was quite tidy and shining again. And last of all Rupert took out apples and nuts and sweets from his sack, and gave some to all the children.

And when St Nicholas had said goodbye and had gone out again into the starlit night, with Rupert skipping behind him and waving his empty sack and his stick and his birch-twig broom, Sylvia and Joan and Terry and Rosaleen and Margaret and Stephen and Luke all sat down on the carpet again in a circle, and hugged their gifts, and talked about St Nicholas, and laughed and enjoyed Rupert's funny, playful punishments all over again.

And then Sylvia begged:

"Mother, please tell us a story about St Nicholas!"

And Joan and Terry and Rosaleen and Margaret and Stephen and Luke all echoed eagerly:

"Oh yes, please — a story about St Nicholas!"

So they put out the big lights, and lit two of the candles on the Advent wreath, and sat in a circle in the firelight while Sylvia's mother told them the Story of Bella, Sophia and the little Bonita.

And this is it:

The Story of Bella, Sophia
and the Little Bonita

One December, long, long ago, St Nicholas and his black page-boy, Rupert, were journeying about the world, St Nicholas with his golden crook and his golden book, and Rupert with his big stick, and his birch-twig broom, and his bulging sack over his shoulder, and a twinkle in both eyes. And on a starlit night when the snow was on the ground, they came to the Valley of the Sleeping Dragon.

And when Rupert heard the dragon breathing in his sleep, his eyes stopped twinkling, and he ceased his playful pranks, and he said fearfully to St Nicholas:

"Good master, *must* we go through this valley? What if we waken the dragon?"

And St Nicholas answered, soothingly:

"We must go through this valley, Rupert; for it leads to the Plain of the Black Morass, where there are children who would be sad if we did not visit them. But have no fear; this dragon eats only golden boys, not black ones, and nothing wakes him except a golden boy being born."

So, with Rupert going on tiptoe, and keeping very close to St Nicholas, and holding his big stick very firmly in case the dragon awoke by mistake, they came safely through the Valley of the Sleeping Dragon to the Plain of the Black Morass. And before them on the plain shone the lights of a village; and outside the village was a stable, half in ruins; and as they drew near the stable, they could smell peat-smoke and see firelight flickering through the holes in its tumbledown walls.

And Rupert's eyes twinkled in amazement, and he asked:

"Surely, good master, no one lives in this tumble-down stable?"

And St Nicholas replied:

"Yes, an old sick father, who is very poor, lives there with three young daughters, Bella the beautiful, Sophia the wise, and Bonita, who is little and good."

Then Rupert asked:

"What do you need from my sack, good master, to help Bella, Sophia and the little Bonita to overcome their faults?"

Then, standing in the snow and the starlight, St Nicholas opened his big golden book, and turned over its black pages; but the names of Bella, Sophia and the little Bonita did not light up anywhere. Then he turned to the golden pages, and their names lit up, and he read out to Rupert:

"Bella had an enchanted cow, her most treasured possession; and she sold it to buy bread for her sick father. Sophia had a spinning-wheel, her most treasured possession; and she sold it to buy bread for her sick father. The little Bonita had a sturdy ass, her most treasured possession; and she sold it to buy bread for her sick father."

Then Rupert gave a hop, a skip and a jump, and asked:

"What gifts do you need from my sack, good master, to reward Bella, Sophia and the Little Bonita?"

And St Nicholas replied:

"Let us find out what they would like best."

So St Nicholas and Rupert stood quietly in the snow and the starlight outside the stable, and looked in through a hole in the wall. And they saw the peat-fire smouldering on the stable floor; and beside it, on a bed of straw, the old sick father was lying; and around it, on three tree-stumps, sat Bella, Sophia and the little Bonita, drying a long piece of fine white linen.

And St Nicholas and Rupert heard Sophia say:

"This is my last piece, dear sisters. Tomorrow we must sell it to buy bread. And after that, we have nothing left in all the world that we can sell."

Then Bella sighed, and gazed upward, and said:

"The sky is so full of gold tonight — crowded with stars looking down through the holes in our roof. If only it would spare us a little!"

And the little Bonita gazed upwards, too, and said dreamily:

"Yes, just three little pieces of gold would be all we would want, to buy back Bella's enchanted cow to give us milk again, and Sophia's spinning-wheel to spin for us again, and my sturdy ass to fetch peat from the black morass to feed our fire again."

And Bella and Sophia cried together:

"Ah, little Bonita, what a wonderful gift that would be!"

Then St Nicholas, listening outside in the snow and the starlight, whispered to Rupert:

"Rupert, give me quietly these gifts they long for."

So with a hop Rupert set down his sack in the snow, and with a skip he opened it, and with a jump he took out three golden coins and gave them to St Nicholas. And St Nicholas gently tossed them through the hole in the wall; and with a *clink, clink, clink*, they fell on the hearth-stone at the feet of Bella, Sophia and the little Bonita.

And Bella, Sophia and the little Bonita folded the linen quickly, and, wondering, picked them up. And when they saw what each held, they showed each golden coin, rejoicing, to their father, then ran at once to the door, to thank the giver. But St Nicholas and Rupert had disappeared, and were already bringing joy to other children in the village; and Bella, Sophia and the little Bonita found nobody there at all.

So out at once into the snow and the starlight they went happily together, each with her golden coin, to buy back Bella's enchanted cow and Sophia's spinning-wheel and the little Bonita's sturdy ass.

And when they had returned, each with her most treasured possession, and the stable was ringing with their gratitude and joy, there came a sudden knock at the door; and the little Bonita ran and opened it. And outside stood an old bearded man in a tattered cloak, and beside him a lady, spent and weary.

And the old man asked humbly:

"Could we beg for shelter for the night, kind people? The lady is so weary, she can go no further."

Then the old sick father called from his bed of straw:

"Come in and welcome, travellers!"

And they came in thankfully.

Then Sophia made the lady a bed upon the straw; and Bella milked her enchanted cow, and brought milk to the lady and the old man; and the little Bonita took her sturdy ass through the snow and the starlight to the black morass for peat to feed the fire that the lady and the old man might be warmed.

And that night a golden boy was born in the stable.

Then the little Bonita heated water on the peat-fire, and washed the golden boy. And Bella brought milk from her enchanted cow, and gave the golden boy his first earthly nourishment. And Sophia took her last piece of fine linen, which they had been going to sell next day, and tore half of it into strips to make swaddling-bands for the golden boy. And when they took back the golden boy, washed, fed and clothed, to lay him in the lady's arms, they saw she had a sun beaming upon her heart, and a coronet of stars shining upon her hair, and about her waist a silver girdle, with silver fringes reaching to the knee.

And as they gazed in joy and amazement, a new noise broke the silence, like rumbling thunder very far away.

And Bella exclaimed:

"Listen — the dragon is stirring in his sleep! The first ray of the rising sun will waken him. Sophia, Bonita, let us think quickly. How can we save the golden boy?"

And Sophia replied:

"On the other side of the black morass the golden boy will be safe. But he must be there by sunrise."

But the old sick father on his bed of straw said in distress:

"But who can find the way across the black morass by night? One false step and the deep bog would swallow them."

And the little Bonita answered cheerily:

"My sturdy ass can find the way, so often has he been there to fetch peat to feed our fire."

Then Bella gave the old man milk and their last bread for the journey; and Sophia took what was left of her last piece of fine linen, and wrapped it like a white cloak about the golden boy. And the lady thanked them, and seated herself upon the little Bonita's sturdy ass, and took the golden boy into the shelter of her mantle and the warmth of the sun that beamed upon her heart, and with the old man trudging alongside, she rode slowly away across the black morass through the snow and the starlight, while far away in his valley, like a distant thunderstorm, the dragon stirred in his sleep.

And Bella, Sophia and the little Bonita stood at the open door till the lady's coronet of stars could no longer be seen. And when they came again into the stable, their father cried in amazement:

"Bella, Bella! What is beaming on your heart?"

And when Sophia and the little Bonita looked at Bella, they saw that, like the mother of the golden boy, she had a sun beaming from her breast.

And again their father cried in amazement:

"Sophia, Sophia! What is shining on your hair?"

And when Bella and the little Bonita looked at Sophia, they saw that, like the mother of the golden boy, she had a coronet of stars upon her head.

And yet a third time their father cried in amazement:

"Little Bonita, how your girdle glitters!"

And when Bella and Sophia looked at the little Bonita, they saw that, like the mother of the golden boy, she wore a silver girdle, and its silver fringes reached from waist to knee.

Then the little Bonita passed the silver fringes lovingly through her fingers, and cried happily:

"With these I can buy another sturdy ass to fetch peat to feed the fire to warm you all."

But their father said:

"There is no longer any need, my little Bonita. See — I am able to work again myself for my dear daughters!"

And he rose from his bed of straw; and they saw that he was sick no longer, but had been made strong and well.

And Bella, Sophia and the little Bonita rejoiced, and ran to their father, and embraced him.

And the distant thunder ceased; and their father said:

"Listen! The dragon is fast asleep again. The golden boy must already be safe beyond the black morass."

Then they all drank together of the milk from the enchanted cow, and warmed themselves at the peat-fire, and looked up thankfully through the holes in the roof at the sky so full of gold, and lay down in joy to sleep.

The Poem of the Golden Boy

When Sylvia's mother had finished the story, the children sat quite quiet, seeing lovely pictures in the fire, of the golden boy, and Bella with the sun beaming on her heart, and Sophia in her coronet of stars, and the little Bonita with her long-fringed silver girdle, till there came three loud knocks at the door again, and again Sylvia ran to open it.

And this time it was the Old Woodsman, who had come with Blackbird and her cart to take Joan and Terry and Rosaleen and Margaret and Stephen and Luke home again to their mothers.

So up were turned the big lights; and all was hurry and scurry and noise and bustle as Joan and Terry and Rosaleen and Margaret and Stephen and Luke got into their outdoor shoes and their leggings and their scarves and their greatcoats, all telling the Old Woodsman about

St Nicholas and Rupert, all at the same time, and all at the tops of their voices.

Then Joan and Terry and Rosaleen and Margaret and Stephen and Luke collected all their gifts; and as they said goodbye to Sylvia and her mother, they all said it was the most wonderful party they had ever had. Then they all streamed out into the starlight, and the Old Woodsman lifted them one by one on to the soft hay inside the cart, and tucked them in with warm rugs, and laughed his slow, cosy laugh as he threw over them the net he used when he took his pigs to market.

Then every-one called out good-night again; and off went Blackbird, her cart rumbling behind her, her hoofs going *clop — clop — clop*; and the little bursts of laughter from the children under the pig-net grew fainter, and the lantern swinging behind the cart grew smaller till it was as little as a star.

Then Sylvia and her mother went indoors again; and Sylvia felt suddenly so sleepy that she could scarcely keep awake long enough to undress and tumble into bed and put her Wonder-Book on the bedside table beside Rupert's gifts and softly chant her poetry spell:

"Rhyme-Elves, rich in ringing words
Won from winds and waves and birds,
Lisping leaves and rustling rain,
Sing — sing — for me again!"

And it seemed only a moment before it was morning and Sylvia was awake again. And she gazed with quiet joy at the Wonder-Book's new picture of St Nicholas and Rupert in the snow outside the stable. And when she took her Wonder-Book into her mother's bed, this was the new poem her mother read to her:

Dream — dream —
Bella's enchanted cow!
Give down your milk with joy;
The hour is nearing now
When she a golden boy
Gently to earth shall bring
Through your sweet fostering.
Where his bright head has pressed,
A sun beams from her breast.
Dream — dream —
Bella's enchanted cow!

Whirl — whirl —
Sophia's spinning-wheel!
Beneath her careful hands
The flax-thread fills the reel,
To weave soft swaddling-bands
A golden boy to wrap,
Alight upon her lap.
Now on her hair be set
Stars in a coronet.
Whirl — whirl —
Sophia's spinning-wheel!

Plod — plod —
Bonita's sturdy ass!
Far from the dragon's lair,
Beyond the black morass
A golden boy you bear.
Bonita bids you go
Steadfastly through the snow.
Now shall her girdle be
Silver from waist to knee.
Plod — plod —
Bonita's sturdy ass!

Sylvia's Painting

A few days later, the Old Woodsman came with Blackbird to take Sylvia's mother to do her Christmas shopping. While her mother was getting ready, Sylvia ran out with a carrot for Blackbird, and asked the Old Woodsman:

"Please, Mr Woodsman, what do you think my mother would like for my Christmas present?"

The Old Woodsman thought for a moment; then he said:

"I think she might like you to paint her a picture."

Sylvia thought for a moment, too; then she asked:

"Do you think she would like a picture of the first Christmas?"

And the Old Woodsman said heartily:

"I'm sure she would!"

So as soon as Blackbird and the Old Woodsman had gone *clop — clop — clopping* away, taking Sylvia's mother with them, Sylvia ran back into the white cottage, and got out a big sheet of painting paper and her sponge and her brushes and a mug of water and the little glass jars of liquid colours her mother mixed for her.

And first she damped the paper all over with her sponge, to make the paint flow softly; and then she dipped her brush in the jar of heavenly blue, and began to paint the sky.

And as she painted, the tender blue sky grew, and then the bright green grass below it, and then the crib with a gentle yellow light about it, and Mary sitting near the crib in her blue cloak, and on one side the three kings standing in purple robes and enormous crowns, and on the other the shepherds in their brown jerkins running down the hillside and waving their arms and falling over their crooks in their excitement.

Sylvia washed her brush carefully each time before she dipped it in a jar of fresh colour, just as her mother had taught her, so that the colours should be clean and pure. The picture glowed up at Sylvia, and Sylvia glowed down at the picture; and the time flew by till she suddenly heard Blackbird's *clop — clop — clop* returning. She jumped up to put away the picture quickly before her mother came in; and over went the mug of water right across the picture, and sky and grass and crib and kings and shepherds all began to drown before her eyes.

Sylvia sobbed and sobbed, as she tried to drain away that dreadful flood into her sponge; and then her mother's arm was about her, and her mother's voice was saying comfortingly:

"There, there! We'll just brush the water away here, and make the sky a little bluer there, and put the green back into the grass, and look — it's nearly right again already!"

And all the time her other hand was busy with the paint-brush, saving Sylvia's picture.

Then Sylvia dried her tears, and blew hard into her handkerchief, and said:

"Oh, I *did* so want it to be beautiful!"

And her mother replied cheerfully:

"And so it is. You know, Sylvia, whenever you try hard and it doesn't quite come right, it helps if you remember what the lily said to the fir-tree."

And Sylvia asked eagerly, quite forgetting now to cry:

"Oh, Mother, what *did* the lily say? Is it a story?"

So Sylvia's mother took off her outdoor things and sat down by the big log fire; and Sylvia sat on her mother's knee and leaned against her mother's shoulder with her mother's arm warm and strong and comforting about her. And while Sylvia watched the flames leaping, and only sniffed a little now and then and that quite absent-mindedly, her mother told her the Story of the Tree that Dreamt a Flower.

And this is it:

The Story of the Tree that Dreamt a Flower

There was once an Archer, who dwelt among the stars, and whose arrows brought not wounds but a love for all things good and beautiful.

One day be loosed an arrow which fell to Earth on a cold and naked mountain-side, where no plant had ever grown. And the arrow's feathers turned into roots, and the arrow grew into a tree. And this tree was the first fir-tree.

The tree grew straight and upright, pointing to the stars. And as the tree looked up at the stars, she loved them, because they were good and beautiful. So every day she grew taller, for always she longed to reach them.

Now the stones of that desolate place had rejoiced when the green fir-tree came to live among them; but when they saw her yearning always towards the stars, they feared she would grow right away from them.

So the stones cried out to her:

"Do not forget us altogether, dear fir-tree. It is right that you should love the stars; but love Earth a little, too."

And the fir-tree listened, and looked down, and was sorry for the stones imprisoned in the ground, and she sent her roots down deeper to embrace them. And she began to love the stones and the soil a little, as well as the sky and the stars.

97

Then the small creatures who lived on that cold and naked mountain-side, and who longed for shade and shelter, cried out also to the fir-tree:

"Dear fir-tree, do not forget us, either. We are glad that your head should be lifted towards the stars; but will you not lower your arms a little towards Earth, to bring us shade and shelter?"

And the fir-tree listened, and looked down, and was sorry for the small creatures of the mountain-side; and she let her branches droop until the lowest brushed the ground with their outstretched fingers. And the small creatures of the mountain-side crept beneath the fir-tree thankfully, and found shelter there from the storms, and warmth when the nights were cold.

And now, with her straight trunk, and her drooping branches, and her sharp tip pointing to the stars, the fir-tree began to show in her very shape that she was an arrow which had turned into a tree.

And she grew to love Earth more and more, and to take more and more soil into her sap, until presently she was wrapped in bark, and her wood grew to have less and less the softness of a plant, and more and more the hardness of a stone.

And now, where she had dropped her pine-needle leaves to the ground, the sparse soil became gradually richer, so that mosses, and small creeping plants, and presently taller plants, also, began to clothe the naked mountain-side. And water-plants began to grow in the little mountain pools which the rain left between the rocks. And among these was a lily-plant, which looked up in love and wonder at the fir-tree, and listened with delight and longing when the fir-tree spoke of the stars to the stones and the small creatures nestling beneath her boughs.

To them it was all like a wonderful fairy-story; for the

stones, imprisoned in the ground, could not see the sky; and the animals, going on all fours, could not lift their heads high enough to gaze upwards at the stars. And the mosses and the stones and the small creatures and the lily-plant would sigh:

"Oh, if only a star would come down and live among us!"

Now the fir-tree often pondered how this might be brought to pass, for she, too, longed for the stones and the mosses and the small creatures of the mountain-side to be able to share her own joy in the goodness and the beauty of the stars. And one night she had a dream.

In this dream she spoke aloud a magic spell, which called strongly upon a star to come to Earth. And a star came curving like a falling spark out of the sky, and entered her sap. And presently, out through the bark of one of her branches the star broke, enfolded in a bud; and the bud opened into an exquisite, delicately tinted flower with tender petals. And that flower was the most beautiful thing which had yet been born upon the Earth.

For all this happened long, long ago, when the Earth was still very young, and there had never yet been any flowers at all; so that the fir-tree's dream was the first dream of the first flower.

And the lily-plant, looking up in love and wonder at the fir-tree, saw the wonderful pictures of the fir-tree's dream painted on the air about her.

Now when the fir-tree woke, she remembered her dream; and she remembered also the magic spell she had spoken aloud in her dream. And she said to herself:

"Is this then the way to bring down a star to gladden the Earth? Can I make my dream come true?"

So now she spoke aloud again the magic spell of her dream, calling strongly upon a star to come to Earth. And the lily-plant, looking up to her in love and wonder, heard her speak aloud the magic spell.

And, just as in her dream, a star came curving like a falling spark out of the sky, and entered the fir-tree's sap. And presently, again as in her dream, out through the bark of one of her branches broke the star, enfolded in a bud. And the fir-tree trembled with happiness; and the lily-plant, looking up to the fir-tree in love and wonder, trembled with happiness with her.

But what happened next was different from the dream. For the strength and stiffness of the fir-tree's wood entered into the bud, so that this became woody, too. It sat on her branch like a stone, the colour of a stone; and when it opened, it had not the tender delicately tinted petals of the exquisite flower of her dream, but thick, hard scales. It was not a real flower; it was a fir-cone.

And the fir-tree cried in distress:

"I can never make my beautiful dream come true! There is too much soil in my sap."

And she was so sorrowful at her failure that she began to weep. But through her weeping she heard a sweet voice, speaking words of comfort to her from below. And when she looked down, she saw that it was the lily-plant which grew in the mountain pool the rain had made between the rocks.

And the lily-plant said:

"Do not weep, dear fir-tree, for you have done a new and a wonderful thing. You have taught the stars the way to become flowers; and with your leave I and other tender plants can still make your dream come true."

And the fir-tree dried her tears, and answered:

"With all my heart."

So the lily-plant spoke aloud the magic spell which she had learnt from the fir-tree, calling strongly upon a star to come to Earth. And a star came curving like a falling spark out of the sky, and entered the lily-plant's sap.

Now there was no soil in the lily-plant's sap, for she lived with her feet in water, and every part of her was soft and delicate and tender. So now a stem rose from between her leaves, lifting the star aloft, enfolded in a soft bud. And the soft bud opened into a delicately tinted flower with tender petals, as beautiful as the flower in the fir-tree's dream. And this was the first real flower; and the first real flower was a lily. And because the star which had entered the lily-plant's sap was a six-pointed one, the lily had six petals.

And just as the lily-plant, in love and in wonder, had learnt from the fir-tree, so other tender plants learnt from the lily-plant how to call stars down from the sky and turn them into flowers.

And the fir-tree rejoiced to see her dream come true.

And the flower of the lily-plant told her:

"I heard a prophecy among the stars, dear fir-tree, while I was still a star myself before I came to Earth. And this was it: Because you were the first plant to long to bring a star to Earth and give birth to a flower, and because you longed to give this beautiful gift to the stones and the small creatures, the time will come when once every year you will be covered from tip to toe with stars and flowers and gifts and lighted candles. And just as the small mountain creatures love you now, so little children everywhere will love you. You will be the most beautiful and best-loved tree in all the world!"

And that is how the Archer's arrow became the Christmas tree.

The Poem of the Christmas Tree

After the Story of the Tree that Dreamt a Flower, Sylvia went back to her painting comforted and cheered; and instead of being spoilt, the picture came up out of the flood more beautiful than before.

Sylvia took Titania to bed with her that night, to remind her of the story, because Titania had been born a Christmas tree fairy. She put out her Wonder-Book, open at a new page, and softly chanted her poetry spell:

> "Rhyme-Elves, rich in ringing words
> Won from winds and waves and birds,
> Lisping leaves and rustling rain,
> Sing — sing — for me again!"

And when she woke next morning, there on the new page was a new picture, of the fir-tree growing on the naked mountain-side. And when she and Titania took the Wonder-Book into her mother's bed, this was the new poem her mother read to them:

> The Christmas tree
> Sets in the crystal snow
> The warmth of candle-glow.

> The Christmas tree
> In winter's shivering gloom
> Makes fire-red roses bloom.

> The Christmas tree
> Be-diamonds with its light
> December's darkest night.

The Christmas tree
In the sun's feeblest hour
Brings barren boughs to flower.

The Christmas tree
For all this waiting Earth
Brings Christmas stars to birth.

Star, rose and candle be
Gifts on each Christmas tree!

Getting Ready for Christmas

When Sylvia's mother had read the Poem of the Christmas Tree to Sylvia and Titania, she asked:

"Would you like us to go and see the Old Woodsman today, Sylvia, and choose *your* Christmas tree?"

Sylvia jumped with joy at this; and soon after breakfast she and her mother set off along the woodland path. Before long they saw the Old Woodsman at work among his trees; and Sylvia ran to throw her arms round his shiny corduroy knees in greeting. He took them round his nursery of young fir-trees, and Sylvia found it very difficult to choose her Christmas tree, because she would have liked them all to have the joy of being covered from tip to toe with stars and roses and gifts and lighted candles.

And the Old Woodsman said:

"Of course each fir-tree hopes it will be the one you choose, because every fir-tree longs to go inside a house and share Christmas with a child. But those that stay out in the starlight will have *their* Christmas too, with the snow to cover them and the wind to tell them stories."

So Sylvia felt happier about them, and chose one which was just as high as herself; and the Old Woodsman promised to bring it to the white cottage on Christmas Eve, and to dig it up carefully and not hurt its roots, so that when Christmas was over, Sylvia could plant it in her garden beside the fairy tree.

So now Sylvia counted the days till Christmas Eve; and how they fled by, filled with getting ready for Christmas! There were all the presents to finish making, and to wrap in coloured paper and tie with coloured ribbon, for her mother and the Old Woodsman and Joan and Terry and

Rosaleen and Margaret and Luke and Stephen. There were biscuits to be cut into trees and stars and flowers and hearts and crescent moons out of big sheets of sugar-frosted pastry with the cutters St Nicholas had given her. There were mince pies to make; and the Christmas pudding and the Christmas cake and Sylvia's birthday cake, as well, to be mixed and stirred and baked and iced. And there were moon and star candle-holders to be made out of acorn-cups and beech-nut cups, and gilded with gold paint; and baskets to hold rainbow-coloured sweets to be made out of gold paper.

And every evening, after all this busyness, there was the quiet time in the firelight with her mother, practising carols while the candles on the Advent wreath — first three, then all four of them — shone softly in the darkness.

And now at last came Christmas Eve; and after lunch the Old Woodsman arrived, with a cluster of holly berries in his hat and another on Blackbird's bridle. He brought Sylvia's fir-tree and a big armful of holly and a little bunch of the mistletoe which grew on his old apple-tree. And when he had carried the tree-tub into a corner of the living-room and put soil into it, he and Sylvia and Sylvia's mother planted the Christmas tree in it together.

And when the Old Woodsman and Blackbird had gone on to the village, with Blackbird's cart full of holly and mistletoe and Christmas trees for Joan and Terry and Rosaleen and Margaret and Stephen and Luke, Sylvia and her mother put the holly round the room; and then came the lovely, lovely task of decorating the Christmas tree.

There were thirty-three red roses and thirty-three white candles to fasten on its branches, and golden stars and golden sweet-baskets and apples and oranges; and there were all the gifts in their coloured wrappings to pile on the floor below. And last of all, Sylvia laid silver lengths of frosty tinsel over all the boughs.

By now it was growing dusk, so Sylvia's mother lit the four candles on the Advent wreath, then gave Sylvia the taper; and very, very carefully, and holding her breath all the while, Sylvia lit, one by one, all the thirty-three white candles on the Christmas tree.

And when she stood back to look at it, shining and shimmering and glimmering and glittering in the candle-light, it was so beautiful that she could only stare and stare. Everything on the tree shone softly back at her with gentle lights and colours and gleams of gold and silver; and Sylvia sat down on the hearthrug, and leaned against her mother's knee, and stared and stared at the lighted tree, drinking its gentle beauty in.

And presently she murmured:

"I wonder if there's ever been *anyone* as beautiful as a Christmas tree?"

And her mother smiled and answered:

"I think the kind Cordita must have been!"

And Sylvia begged:

"Oh, Mother, do tell me about her!"

So, sitting in the firelight and the candle-light, with the tree shining softly in all its gentle glory, Sylvia's mother told Sylvia this story, the Story of Cordita and the Three Little Men:

The Story of Cordita and the Three Little Men

There was once a king who had one dearly beloved son. When this prince was born, his fairy godmothers gathered round his cradle, and each gave him a gift. One said he should be handsome; one said he should be good; one said he should marry the kindest maiden in the kingdom; one said that summer's golden bird should fly about this maiden's head; and one said that a shower of gems should fall from her lips each time she spoke.

And when all except the last of the fairy godmothers had spoken, a wicked fairy appeared beside the cradle; and she cried triumphantly:

"In spite of all your promises, the prince shall be deceived, and shall marry the wrong maiden."

Then the king turned in dismay to the last fairy godmother, and begged her:

"Can you not lift this curse from my beloved child?"

And the last fairy godmother answered:

"I cannot destroy the curse entirely; but I will give the prince this gift with which to meet its danger — that in silence he shall find wisdom."

The years passed, and the young prince came to an age when he should marry. And the king announced throughout his kingdom that if anywhere there was a maiden about whose head flew summer's golden bird and from whose lips fell a shower of gems each time she spoke, a messenger was to be sent at once to the royal palace. But the weeks went by, and the months went by, and there came no messenger.

Now on the other side of the mountains from the royal palace there lived a beautiful maiden named Cordita, who was all alone in the world except for her cruel step-mother and her ugly step-sister, who was called Kapala. They made Cordita work hard all day in the kitchen, and gave her nothing but rags to wear; and all she was given to eat was a dry crust of bread in the evening, and at night they made her sleep in the loft over the stable. But Cordita was so gentle that she bore it all without complaining.

One bitter winter's night she was trudging wearily across the courtyard to her bed among the straw in the loft, carrying her crust of bread in one hand and her lighted lantern in the other, when suddenly she heard three faint, whimpering calls for help. She was so kind-hearted that although the icy wind was cutting through her thin rags and the snow bit her bare feet at every step, she had to pause and search; and at last, beside the well in the middle of the courtyard, she found three little men imprisoned in a block of ice, where they were slowly freezing to death.

And Cordita cried in distress for them:

"Oh, you poor little men! Just wait while I find a stone to break the ice!"

And she groped about in the deep snow till she found a stone. But though she hammered with all her might, the block of ice remained unbroken.

Then the first little man called out to her through the ice:

"Kind Cordita, the ice would melt if a fire were lit beside it. Do you think you could do that?"

And the kind Cordita answered:

"I will do that gladly."

And she broke off twigs from the bare branches of the lime-tree which grew over the well; and she opened her lantern and took out the lighted candle and tried to light the twigs with it. But the twigs would not catch fire.

Then the second little man called out to her through the ice:

"Kind Cordita, the fire could be kindled by a drop of blood given by a maiden out of her own heart. Do you think you could do that?"

And the kind Cordita answered:

"I will do that gladly."

And she arranged the twigs across the lighted candle, and opened the rags on her bosom, and pricked herself with a pin; and a drop of blood fell down on to the twigs. And at once a rose-red flame shot up, and the twigs began to burn, and the ice began to melt, and — hey presto! — there stood the three little men, released from their imprisonment.

And when they had all three thanked her, the third little man went on:

"Kind Cordita, we are hungry. Could you spare us a little bread?"

And the kind Cordita answered:

"I will do that gladly. Come with me into the shelter of the stable."

And she opened the stable-door and led them in, and set down her lantern, and they all sat round it. And she broke her crust of bread into four pieces, and she and the three little men ate her day's food together.

And when they had finished eating, the first little man said:

"In reward for Cordita's kindness, I will give her a gift. As soon as tomorrow's sun rises, summer's golden bird shall fly about her head."

And the second little man said:

"In reward for Cordita's kindness, I too will give her a gift. From the first question she answers tomorrow, a shower of gems shall fall from her lips each time she speaks."

And the third little man said:

"In reward for Cordita's kindness, I also will give her a gift. When a white horse has spent three nights in this stable, a king's son shall make her his bride."

And Cordita thanked them shyly. And the very next moment, all three little men had vanished.

When Cordita came out of the stable next morning to begin her long day's work, the sun was just rising; and as its first ray touched her, summer's golden bird began to fly about her head. And with every step she took, the snow melted; and the harsh wind grew soft and warm; and the whole courtyard was filled with flowers; and the lime-tree over the well was covered with blossom and with bees humming in the blossom; and the bare bushes in the corners of the courtyard broke into green leaf, and from their branches birds began to sing.

And the bird-song was so loud and joyous that it sounded through the house and woke Kapala from her sleep; and she left her bed and went to the window to see what was the matter. And in the courtyard below she saw the blossoming lime-tree, and beneath it Cordita drawing water from the well; and about Cordita's head a golden bird was flying.

And as soon as she saw it, she wanted the golden bird for herself, and was angry that Cordita should own anything so beautiful. So she ran to her sleeping mother, and shook her awake, and shouted:

"Mother, Cordita has a wonderful golden bird. Take it away from her and give it to me!"

And her mother rose from her bed and went to the window, and stood amazed at the bird-song and the humming of the bees and the melting of the snow and the warm wind and the blossoming lime-tree and the courtyard full of flowers. And when she saw Cordita drawing water from the well with summer's golden bird flying about her head, she dressed quickly and went down into the courtyard, and asked Cordita sharply:

"Cordita, where did that golden bird come from?"

And Cordita answered modestly:

"There were three little men in the courtyard last night, Step-mother, and the golden bird was a gift from one of them."

And as she spoke, a shower of gems fell from her lips.

And the step-mother stared at the gems sparkling

among the flowers, and greedily gathered them up, and sharply asked again:

"And who gave you *this* gift, Cordita?"

And again Cordita answered modestly:

"Another of the little men, Step-mother."

And again a shower of gems fell from her lips.

And when the step-mother had greedily gathered these, also, again she asked sharply:

"And pray, what did the third one give you?"

And Cordita blushed and answered shyly:

"He promised that a king's son should make me his bride."

And again a shower of gems fell from her lips.

And as soon as the step-mother heard this, she said to herself as she gathered these gems, also:

"How can I make the king's son marry Kapala instead?"

And she began to plot and plan how she could bring this about.

And she caught the golden bird roughly in her two hands, and called Kapala to hold him tightly while she tied a strong cord about his leg; and the other end of the cord she fastened firmly to a lock of Kapala's hair. And every time that Cordita spoke, her step-mother greedily gathered up the shower of gems which fell from her lips, and hoarded them in a great iron chest.

And she sent a messenger on a swift horse across the snowy mountain to the royal palace. And when he was brought into the king's presence, he knelt and gave this message:

"O King, my mistress bids me say that though snow lies deep everywhere else in your kingdom, in her courtyard it is summer; and summer's golden bird flies round her daughter's head; and from her daughter's lips falls a shower of gems each time she speaks."

112

And the king questioned the messenger as to the truth of the message; and the messenger replied:

"O King, with my own eyes I have seen the lime-tree blossoming in the courtyard, and the golden bird flying about the maiden's head; and my mistress has shown me a great iron chest filled with the gems that have fallen from her daughter's lips."

Then the king rejoiced greatly. But he had not forgotten the wicked fairy's curse. So he sent the messenger back on his swift horse with this message:

"The king's son will come himself to spend three days with this maiden. And if at the end of three days his heart is content, he will bring her back to the royal palace and make her his bride."

And he called his son to him, and said:

"My son, make ready to go and spend three days with this maiden. I send you alone, for only your own heart can tell whether this is your godmother's choice or the fairy curse at work. But take these three gifts; give the golden shoes to her after the first night, and the golden comb after the second; they will help you to decide whether she is the false bride or the true. And if your heart is content, give her the golden dress after the third night; but if your heart is not content, remember your godmother's promise that in silence you will find wisdom."

Then the king's son took the three gifts, and embraced his father, and saddled his white horse, and set off alone across the snowy mountain.

Meanwhile the messenger had returned to the stepmother, and given her the king's message. And her evil heart rejoiced; and she dressed Kapala in her richest garments; and she warned her:

"Do not speak one single word to the king's son; you have only to be careful for three days, and you will be a princess for the rest of your life."

And to Cordita the step-mother said:

"Keep out of sight while the king's son is here. You are never to leave the kitchen except to go to your loft at night."

So Cordita did not see the king's son arrive, riding his white horse.

As he entered the courtyard and saw it filled with flowers though the snow still lay deep around, and saw the lime-tree covered with blossom, and heard the singing of the birds and the humming of the bees, and felt the soft warm wind, his heart leapt in his breast, and he said to himself:

"Yes, surely here I shall find the bride of my god-mother's choice!"

But when the step-mother met him and brought him into the house and presented Kapala to him, he was perplexed; for he had thought his bride would be beautiful, whereas Kapala was ill-favoured; and the golden bird was not flying happily round her head, as he had expected, but was beating its wings as if trying to escape. And he wondered to himself:

"Can this really be the kindest maiden in my father's kingdom, with that ill-tempered mouth?"

But he greeted her courteously; and when she curtsied but spoke no word in answer, her mother quickly explained:

"Your Royal Highness, my daughter is so overcome with joy at your arrival that for the time being it has robbed her of her voice. But come with me and I will show you the gems which fall from her lips when she speaks."

And she opened the great iron chest, and showed him the gems which had fallen from Cordita's lips.

And the king's son was more than ever perplexed; but he remembered that in silence he would find wisdom, so he said nothing of his thoughts, but graciously took his place at the feast Cordita had worked hard all day preparing for him.

After that long day's work Cordita was very weary that night as she trudged across the courtyard to her bed in the loft, her crust of bread in one hand and her lantern in the other. But when she opened the stable-door, her weariness fell from her; for the light of her lantern fell on a magnificent white horse. She ran forward happily, and hung the lantern on a nail above his stall, and laid her cheek against his glossy neck, and murmured:

"Rest and be refreshed, beautiful white one! Three nights in the stable, and the king's son will make me his bride!"

And as she spoke, a shower of gems fell from her lips, and were caught, sparkling, in the white horse's mane.

Then Cordita shared her crust of bread with the white horse, and took her lantern from the nail, and climbed up to her bed among the straw in the loft, and quickly went to sleep.

Next morning the king's son brought the golden shoes to Kapala, as his father had instructed him to do. And they were so rich and costly that Kapala pounced on them greedily, and quite forgot her mother's warning, and exclaimed:

"How fine I shall look in these!"

And the king's son noticed that her lost voice had returned, and he watched for the shower of gems to fall from her lips; but there was no shower of gems. But he remembered that it was in silence that he would find wisdom; so again he held his peace.

After breakfast he went to the stable to visit his white horse; and there, caught in the white horse's mane, a shower of gems was sparkling. And again he wondered, and still he held his peace. But that night he withdrew earlier from the feast, and hid himself in the shadows in the corner of the stable.

And presently the door opened, and in came Cordita, her crust of bread in one hand and her lantern in the other. She hung the lantern on the nail above the white horse's stall, and as its light fell on her, her beauty shone through her rags, so that again the king's son felt his heart leap in his breast.

And Cordita laid her cheek against the white horse's glossy neck, and murmured:

"Rest and be refreshed, beautiful white one! Two nights in the stable, and the king's son will make me his bride!"

And as she spoke, a shower of gems fell from her lips, and were caught, sparkling, in the white horse's mane.

Then again Cordita shared her crust of bread with the white horse, and took her lantern from the nail, and climbed up to her bed among the straw in the loft, and quickly went to sleep.

And the king's son watched her go and held his peace.

Next morning the king's son brought the golden comb to Kapala, as his father had instructed him to do. And it was so beautiful that she pounced on it greedily, and began at once to comb her hair with it. And before she realised what was happening, she had combed the knotted cord right off the lock of hair to which her mother had fastened it, and freed the golden bird; and with a trill of joy it rose in the air, and darted through the window, and was lost to view. And still the king's son held his peace.

And that night again he withdrew early from the feast, and hid himself in the shadows in the corner of the stable. And presently the door opened, and in came Cordita, her crust of bread in one hand and her lantern in the other. And as she hung the lantern on the nail above the horse's stall, the king's son saw that the golden bird was flying

116

117

happily about her head, with Kapala's loose cord still swinging from its leg.

And Cordita said to the golden bird:

"Come to my hand, beautiful golden one, that I may free you from that cord."

And she held out her hand, and the golden bird came to it, and she set the bird down gently on the white horse's back, and freed its leg from the cord. And the shower of gems which had fallen from her lips were caught, sparkling, in the white horse's mane.

And Cordita laid her cheek against the white horse's glossy neck, and murmured:

"Rest and be refreshed, beautiful white one! One night in the stable, and the king's son will make me his bride!"

And again a shower of gems fell sparkling from her lips.

Then Cordita shared her crust of bread with the white horse and the golden bird, and took her lantern from the nail, and climbed up to her bed among the straw in the loft, and quickly went to sleep. And the king's son stole from the stable, and fetched the golden dress, and climbed softly up to the loft, and spread the golden dress on the straw beside the sleeping Cordita. For in silence he had found wisdom; and he knew now who was to be his true bride.

And at sunrise next morning, when Cordita awoke, she found the golden dress gleaming on the straw beside her. And she rose, and drew water from the well, and bathed herself, and put on the golden dress. And when she came forth from the stable in the golden dress, her feet still bare and summer's golden bird flying free about her head, the king's son was waiting under the blossoming lime-tree; and without a word he took her hand and led her into the house.

Now for once the step-mother and Kapala had also risen at sunrise, for the step-mother hoped that this morning the king's son would bring Kapala the golden dress and ride away with her to the royal palace to make her his bride. But when they heard the door open, and turned to find Cordita standing shyly there, wearing the golden dress, her hand in the hand of the king's son, and summer's golden bird flying about her head, they knew that the prince had found his true bride in spite of all their plotting, and they could find no word to say for guilt and shame.

Then the king's son said, his hand still holding Cordita's:

"I have found the maiden of my godmother's promise. Cordita, will you come home with me to my father's palace and be my bride?"

And Cordita answered softly:

"I will do that gladly."

Then Kapala brought the golden shoes and the golden comb to Cordita; and the step-mother opened the iron chest for her to take the gems; and they both begged her to forgive them.

And Cordita answered gently:

"I will do that gladly. The golden shoes and the golden comb I will take, because they are bride-gifts; but the gems are for you to keep, and may you both live long and be happy."

And when Cordita had put on the golden shoes and combed her hair with the golden comb, she looked every inch a princess. And they went hand-in-hand across the flowering courtyard amid the birdsong to the stable; and the king's son lifted Cordita on to the white horse in front of him, and held her safely there; and they set out together on their journey over the snowy mountain.

And summer's golden bird flew with them, so that all along their path the snow melted, and the harsh wind grew soft and warm, and flowers sprang up, and bare bushes burst into green leaf, and on their branches birds began to sing. And every time Cordita spoke, a shower of gems fell from her lips to sparkle among the flowers.

And when they reached the royal palace, the king welcomed Cordita as a dearly beloved daughter, and a great banquet was prepared, and the prince made her his bride. And they lived together in great loving-kindness.

And when the king grew old and died, the prince and Cordita ruled the kingdom together in gentleness and joy; and wherever Cordita went, the golden bird flew about her head, so that summer always went with her; and there was no poverty anywhere in the kingdom because of the shower of gems which fell from her lips each time she spoke. And all the people loved their beautiful queen; and they called her everywhere the kind Cordita.

The Poem of the Kind Cordita

Early next morning Sylvia woke to the sound of distant bells ringing "Christ-mass! Christ-mass! Christ-mass!"

She bounded up in bed; and first she explored the treasures in her stocking — fruit, nuts, chocolate, toys, new gleaming shillings, and, hiding away in the toe, a shy little white sugar mouse.

And as she turned to put her treasures on the table at her bedside, there lay the Wonder-Book, open at a new page.

Now Sylvia had longed last night to ask the Rhyme-Elves to paint her a poem about Cordita; but she had felt shy, because it was Christmas Eve, and it was a little like asking them for a Christmas gift. So she had gone to sleep without putting out her Wonder-Book or saying her poetry spell. But they must have come in spite of not being called, and they must have charmed the Wonder-Book from under her pillow while she slept; for there, on a new page, *was* their Christmas gift, after all, with a picture of the three little men imprisoned in the block of ice, with the kind Cordita kindling a fire to release them.

When Sylvia had gathered all her treasures in her arms, and her present for her mother, and her Wonder-Book as well, she went on tiptoe to her mother's door. There she stood and sang a carol very softly; then called out very loudly:

"A happy Christmas, Mother!"

Then she went in, and gave her mother a special Christmas hug and the picture she had painted for her, and climbed into bed beside her.

And when they had looked together at Sylvia's picture of the first Christmas, and her mother had thanked her for it, Sylvia showed her mother all her treasures; and then she opened the Wonder-Book, and exclaimed:

"Mother, what do you think? I didn't ask the Rhyme-Elves for a poem last night; and yet, look — they've written me one!"

Then Sylvia's mother said a very funny thing. She said:

"What do I think, Sylvia? I think you must have a tooth loose!"

Sylvia opened her mouth wide and tapped all along her teeth (both rows); and she found that there actually was one, in the middle at the top, that *was* the least bit shaky!

And she gasped with surprise:

"I *have*! Look! Oh, Mother, how did you guess?"

And her mother explained:

"I guessed because when the Rhyme-Elves start writing poems without being asked, there usually *is* a tooth nearly ready to come out."

And Sylvia asked:

"And what happens, Mother, when the tooth *does* come out?"

And her mother answered:

"Then the Elf-Prince Frey gives you three wonderful gifts; and *then* you can go to school!"

Sylvia bounced up and down on the bed with excitement, and cried, her eyes very big and shining:

"What a lot of lovely things there are waiting to happen to children, aren't there? And wasn't it lucky my tooth came loose just in time for Christmas? Mother, do read me the Rhyme-Elves' Christmas present, please!"

And this was the Rhyme-Elves' Christmas gift to Sylvia, which her mother read to her:

> So kind was Cordita,
> Her heart could kindle fire in snow,
> And cause the iron ice to flow,
> And set cold winter's night aglow.
>
> So kind was Cordita,
> She shared her only crust of bread,
> That hungry fairies might be fed
> And with her love be comforted.
>
> So kind was Cordita,
> About her head flew summer's bird;
> And from her lips with every word
> Fell gems, rejoicing all who heard.
>
> So kind was Cordita,
> A king's son wooed her for his bride,
> And they ruled gently side by side,
> And scattered gladness far and wide.
> So *blest* was Cordita. . . .

Christmas Day

After breakfast Blackbird came *clop — clop — clopping* along the woodland path, for she and the Old Woodsman were to spend Christmas Day with Sylvia and her mother. When the Old Woodsman came into the white cottage, in his Sunday suit and tall starched collar and stiff hat, he looked a little unlike his real, beautiful, shabby work-a-day self; but Sylvia loved him just as much whatever he wore, and came rushing to meet him and hug his knees and wish him a happy Christmas.

And he tossed her up in his arms and kissed her under the mistletoe and gave her a parcel wrapped in scarlet tissue paper; and inside Sylvia found a most beautiful snow-bird, which the Old Woodsman had made of tiny, soft white feathers which wild birds had dropped in the dark wood.

Sylvia cried in delight:

"Oh, Mr Woodsman, I never saw a bird like this before!"

And the Old Woodsman answered in his slow, cosy voice:

"I only saw one once myself. It came to take me to the palace of the Elf-Prince Frey when my first tooth came out."

Then Sylvia asked, excited:

"Will one come for me? *I've* got a loose tooth — look!"

And the Old Woodsman bent down and looked at it solemnly, and said:

"Yes, Sylvia, it looks as if that snow-bird will be coming for you very soon!"

Then Sylvia gave him *her* present, which was a thick round mat of coloured wools which she had made herself for his reading lamp to stand on; and the Old Woodsman admired it tremendously. And then Blackbird and the Old Woodsman took Sylvia *clop — clop — clop* to the village, to give her Christmas gifts to Joan and Terry and Rosaleen and Margaret and Stephen and Luke, and to be given theirs, and to wish all their mothers a happy Christmas, and to invite all her little friends to her birthday party on the last day of the year.

And when they returned, there were all these little friends' gifts to be opened and exclaimed over and played with; and then Christmas dinner to be eaten, with the Old Woodsman enjoying two helpings of the Christmas pudding Sylvia had helped to make; and then the Old Woodsman put on one of Sylvia's mother's aprons, and he and Sylvia washed up together, and he noticed something interesting about the shape of every spoon and the flowers painted on every plate and dish, so that never before had Sylvia realised that washing-up could be so exciting.

And afterwards they all three finished decorating the Christmas cake with bleached almonds and glowing red cherries and pale green strips of angelica, ready for tea. And Sylvia said:

"Our Christmas cake looks so lovely, Mother; do you think I might take Sister-in-the-Bushes a slice, to wish her a happy Christmas?"

And her mother replied:

"Of course you may, Sylvia; though Sisters-in-the-Bushes don't really live on our sort of food, you know."

And Sylvia asked:

"What do they live on, Mother?"

And her mother replied:

"They live on love."

Then Sylvia said:

"Oh, I'll take her lots of that as well. But I wish I knew what to give her for a Christmas present."

And her mother answered:

"I think I know what she would like — to see your Christmas tree."

Then Sylvia asked:

"What shall I say if she wants to give *me* a present, Mother?"

And her mother replied:

"Ask her for a story. Sisters-in-the-Bushes live with the gnomes, and the gnomes know the loveliest and the truest stories in the world."

Then the Old Woodsman helped Sylvia to cut a big slice of the Christmas cake, and Sylvia ran out into the garden with it, and parted the bushes, and called; and Sister-in-the-Bushes came; and they kissed each other and wished each other a happy Christmas; and Sylvia gave Sister-in-the-Bushes the slice of Christmas cake.

And Sister-in-the-Bushes cried:

"How full of goodnesses it is, Sylvia! How the garden birds would love a Christmas feast of it!"

And Sylvia replied with shining eyes:

"Let's give them one together!"

So they broke the slice of cake into tiny pieces and held them out on their palms; and Sister-in-the-Bushes made soft sounds which the birds seemed to understand, for from all parts of the garden, and even from the dark wood beyond the nut-hedge, they came flocking, and folded their wings, and alighted on both children's heads and shoulders.

And when the last crumb was finished, the birds piped little winter songs as they spread their wings and flew away. And Sister-in-the-Bushes said that they were saying:

"Thank you for our Christmas feast, and a happy Christmas, Sylvia!"

Then Sylvia asked Sister-in-the-Bushes:

"Will you come into our white cottage, and see my

Christmas tree, and help me light the candles? I know you don't like houses, but do come just this once!"

And Sylvia took her hand, and drew her through the garden in through the cottage door and into the dusky tree-room. And she lit two tapers at the log fire, and gave one to Sister-in-the-Bushes; and together they went to the tree, each with her lighted taper, and lit the candles one by one till all thirty-three were alight.

Then they sat down on the hearth-rug before the blazing fire, and Sister-in-the-Bushes stared and stared with eyes big and round and full of wonder at the softly shining tree, with its stars and its roses and its candles and its tinsel and its golden baskets and its rosy apples and piled up beneath its branches all the presents for Sylvia's birthday party in their coloured wrappings. And she sighed:

"Oh, Sylvia, you couldn't have given me a lovelier Christmas gift! There isn't anything half so lovely that I can give to you!"

And Sylvia answered quickly:

"Oh, but Mother says there is. She says you know the loveliest and the truest stories in the world. Would you tell me one of them, please?"

So while Sylvia and Sister-in-the-Bushes sat together in the firelight, and the candle-lit tree shone softly on them from its corner, and Sister-in-the-Bushes feasted her wondering eyes on its beauty, she told Sylvia the Story of the Apple-tree that bore a Star:

The Story of the Apple-Tree
that Bore a Star

Long, long, long ago, Father Adam and Mother Eva lived in a Green Garden on the top of the highest mountain in the world. In the Green Garden the flowers never died, and the trees bore fruit every day of the year, and the birds sang wonderful songs in human voices, and all the animals except one were white, and even lions and tigers were as gentle and friendly as lambs.

Father Adam and Mother Eva could eat all the fruit they wanted from any of the trees except one. This was the most beautiful tree of all, with a trunk of clear crystal, leaves of shining silver, and apples of pure gold.

Now the one animal who was not white was a serpent, and he was coloured like a flame. He did not really belong in the Green Garden, for the Moon was his real home. And one day he came to Mother Eva and said:

"Look at those golden apples, Eva. Are they not the most beautiful fruits in the whole Green Garden?"

And Mother Eva looked and said they were.

Then the Moon-Serpent said again:

"No fruit in the whole Green Garden tastes as sweet as they do. No fruit in the whole Green Garden is so juicy and refreshing. Why do you not eat one of these golden apples, Eva?"

And Mother Eva answered:

"Father Adam and I may eat of all the other fruits in the Green Garden; but of these we may not eat."

And the Moon-Serpent asked:

"But would you not *like* to eat one of these golden apples, Eva?"

And Mother Eva looked longingly at the golden apples and said she would.

Then the Moon-Serpent began to sing:

"Take and eat, Eva! Eva, take and eat!"

And he wove a spell round Mother Eva with his long, flaming folds.

And his enchantments worked on Mother Eva, and she stretched out her hand and plucked one of the golden apples; and it lay ripe and warm and glowing in her palm.

And she went to Father Adam, and she said:

"Look, Adam — a golden apple from the tree with the trunk of clear crystal and the leaves of shining silver! I am going to eat of it. Eat with me!"

Now Father Adam would never himself have taken a golden apple from the tree. But when he saw one lying ripe and warm and glowing in Mother Eva's hand, and when he saw her bite it and draw in her breath with pleasure at its taste, and when she held it out for him to bite, Father Adam ate of the golden apple, too.

And a great darkness fell; and when the darkness lifted, they found they were outside the door of the Green Garden, on the bare mountain-side, and a Shining One was guarding the door with a great sword of fire.

And there stood Father Adam with a heavy heart, and stared sorrowfully back at the Green Garden. And there stood Mother Eva, weeping, with the half-eaten golden apple in her hand.

And from everywhere around them came the sound of weeping, too; for when the golden apple was eaten, the whole Earth was stricken sore. So soil and stone and crystal, and root and leaf and flower, and river and rain and dewdrop, and air and wind and light and fire, all wept.

And now for the first time clouds hid the sun; and flowers died; and cold and darkness came where all had been warmth and light; and the birds no longer sang in human voices; and the white, gentle beasts snarled and killed each other and grew fiercely coloured coats.

And Father Adam said to the Shining One with the sword of fire who guarded the door of the Green Garden:

"Must we stay outside for ever and ever, O Shining One? May we *never* come again into the Green Garden?"

And the Shining One with the sword of fire replied:

"Never will my sword of fire be blown aside from the door of the Green Garden till the tree which grows from the core of the golden apple in Eva's hand shall bear a star for fruit."

So Father Adam and Mother Eva went sadly down the mountain-side; and in the valley below they found a cave in which to live. And outside the cave Mother Eva planted the core of the golden apple; and the next year a tiny tree began to grow from it.

Year by year Father Adam and Mother Eva watched anxiously as the little tree grew larger. Its trunk was not of clear crystal, like that of the tree in the Green Garden, but black and rough to the touch; and its leaves were not leaves of shining silver, but leaves which withered and fell off and left the branches bare.

When the little tree grew big enough to bear fruit, Mother Eva sat by it night and day to watch it bear a star. But instead it bore an apple, not even a golden apple like the apple the seed had come from, not an apple sweet and juicy and refreshing, like those in the Green Garden, but a green apple, a sour apple, an apple which could go bad.

And as the years went by, hundreds and hundreds of years, the trunk grew rougher, and the leaves grew more withered, and the apples grew smaller and harder and greener and sourer, till the time came when anyone who ate them was ill for ever after.

Now in the days before Mother Eva plucked the golden apple, if you had looked at the Earth from one of the stars you would have seen that the Earth was a star, too, sending out starlight and singing, as the other stars still do. But after Mother Eva had plucked the apple, the Earth began to lose its light and forget its song. And the sourer the apples grew, the darker and the more silent became this star of Earth, till the time came when the other stars looked for its light and could see only darkness, and listened for its song and found it had become completely dumb.

And they knew that there was one thing only that could help the dark and silent Earth. And that would be the coming of the Christmas Child.

So the Christmas Child began his journey down through the vast golden sky, journeying on his own five-pointed golden star, enfolded in a great five-petalled flower of light shaped like a white wild rose.

And as he approached the Earth, the earthly mother and father to whom he was coming were on a journey, too. And when night came on they had nowhere to sleep except a cave; and this was the very same cave as that in which Father Adam and Mother Eva had lived when they came down the mountain-side from the Green Garden. And outside the cave was still growing Mother Eva's sour apple-tree.

And at midnight the Christmas Child reached the Earth; and as he entered the cave to be born, he hung his five-pointed golden star enfolded in its white five-petalled rose of light on the top bough of the apple-tree, where one hard, sour, withered apple was still clinging. And the star, enfolded in its flower, sank into the hard, sour, withered apple; and the apple grew firm and rosy and sweet and juicy and refreshing; and never again was anyone who ate apples from that tree ill for ever after.

And at the same moment the Earth felt a lessening of that pain which had lasted ever since Mother Eva plucked the golden apple. And soil and stone and crystal, and root and leaf and flower, and river and rain and dewdrop, and air and wind and light and fire, all began to rejoice.

And the other stars, as they looked towards the Earth, saw it begin very faintly to shine again. And when they listened hard they could hear it beginning very softly to sing its own song again.

And the Shining One who guarded the door of the Green Garden felt a gentle wind arise, blowing his fiery sword backward, and he knew that the time had come when the apple-tree outside the cave had borne a star for fruit.

And if you cut a thin strip crossways from an apple and hold it to the light, you will see in the middle of it a five-pointed star within a white wild rose. And this can remind you that at the coming of the Christmas Child the pangs of Earth were lightened, and Earth began to shine and sing again, and the sword of fire was blown aside before the door of the Green Garden.

The Poem of Eva's Apple

When Sister-in-the-Bushes had slipped back into the garden, and Sylvia and her mother and the Old Woodsman had had tea and were sitting together round the fire, with the candles on the Advent wreath and on the Christmas tree all lit, Sylvia brought a large, round, rosy apple to the Old Woodsman, and stood between his knees, and said to him:

"Please, Mr Woodsman, will you show me the star and the flower inside the apple?"

And the Old Woodsman seemed to know all about it, for he took out his pocket-knife and he cut the apple in half — not down, the way you usually do cut an apple, but straight across the core. And already Sylvia could see that when you cut an apple this way the core is the shape of a five-pointed star. And then the Old Woodsman cut the apple right across again, and gave Sylvia the very thinnest slice you could imagine taken from right across the middle of the apple, with a thin red line of rosy skin encircling it.

And the Old Woodsman said:

"Now hold it to the light!"

And when Sylvia held it up beneath the Advent candles, it was so thin that the light came shining through, and she saw just what Sister-in-the-Bushes had described; for enfolding the core's five-pointed star there was a white, five-petalled flower, just the shape of a wild rose, showing very faintly in the apple's creamy flesh.

And Sylvia held it up for her mother to see, and cried:

"Isn't it wonderful, Mother — when you eat an apple, you eat a flower and a star as well!"

And she went to bed that night with her heart still full of this wonder; so that it did not seem at all surprising that when she woke next morning the new picture on a new page of her Wonder-Book should be one of Father Adam and Mother Eva and the Shining One with the sword of fire outside the door of the Green Garden, nor that when she took her Wonder-Book into her mother's bed this should be the new poem that her mother read to her:

Eva plucked the apple,
And Earth was stricken sore;
The sword of flame was flickering
At the Green Garden's door
As she came down the mountain,
Carrying the apple's core.

Eva plucked the apple,
And Earth's starlight paled;
Eva plucked the apple,
And Earth's music failed;
And soil and stone and crystal
And rain and river wailed.

Eva's tree bore apples
Withered, hard and sour,
Till upon its branches
At the first Christmas hour
A golden star descended,
Enfolded in a flower.

Now Earth's pangs are lightened;
The sword's fire backward blows;
Again is heard Earth's music;
Again Earth's starlight glows.
There's a rose within the apple;
There's a star within the rose.

Sylvia's Birthday Poem

Each afternoon on the first five days after Christmas, Sister-in-the-Bushes came into the white cottage at dusk to help Sylvia light the candles on the Christmas tree, and to gaze happily at its beauty while they sat and talked beside the big log fire. And on the fifth afternoon Sylvia said:

"Did you know, Sister-in-the-Bushes, that tomorrow will be the last day of the year?"

And Sister-in-the-Bushes answered, smiling:

"Yes; and it will be your birthday, too, won't it, Sylvia?"

And Sylvia opened her eyes wide, and asked:

"How did you know?"

And Sister-in-the-Bushes smiled again, and answered:

"I remember you being born. It was seven years ago."

Then Sylvia opened her eyes still wider, and begged:

"Oh, do tell me about when I was born. Did I come down on a golden star in a flower of light, like the Christmas Child?"

And Sister-in-the-Bushes answered:

"You came on a rainbow shell shaped like a crescent moon. It sailed away from the full moon and brought you down to Earth. And tomorrow, when you are seven, a silver bell will ring to call it back, but it will leave you here to go on learning how to live on the Earth."

Sylvia thought about this quietly for a few moments. Then she asked:

"But I did have a star of my own when I was born, didn't I, Sister-in-the-Bushes?"

And Sister-in-the-Bushes replied:

"Of course you did, Sylvia. It shone high in the sky, right

over your white cottage; and it sent down a long, rosy ray to warm you; and on the rosy ray your name was written; and that was how your mother knew what name to call you."

And Sylvia asked:

"Will my star do anything new tomorrow, like my moon-boat?"

And Sister-in-the-Bushes replied:

"Indeed it will. It has been waiting for you to be seven so that it can leap the bar of the wide blue air and come closer, to light your earthly way for you and guide you where you ought to go."

Sylvia thought about this quietly, too, for a few moments. Then she asked:

"Did I have any fairy godmothers, Sister-in-the-Bushes, like Cordita's prince?"

And Sister-in-the-Bushes answered:

"Yes, Sylvia, you had twelve. And as you lay in your cradle, they all came and stood round it, and blessed you as you lay asleep; and each of them gave you a gift."

And Sylvia asked:

"And what will *they* do on my birthday?"

And Sister-in-the-Bushes told her:

"Tonight, when you are in bed, they will stand round you in their magic ring again, and bless you as you lie asleep again, and bring you fresh fairy graces because you are seven years old."

And Sylvia exclaimed:

"What wonderful things are going to happen tonight, Sister-in-the-Bushes! I think I'll stay awake, so that I can watch my fairy godmothers standing round my bed, and hear the silver bell call back my moon-boat, and see my star leap down out of the sky."

But that night Sylvia went to bed so happily tired that, try as she would, she simply could *not* keep awake. And so she did not hear the silver bell call back her moon-boat, nor see her star leap down out of the sky, nor watch her fairy godmothers standing round her bed, after all.

But when she woke next morning, there on her bedside table was her mother's birthday gift — a beautiful new Wonder-Book all ready for next year, with three hundred and sixty five big empty white pages, and with golden flowers and birds tooled on its blue leather covers. And the old Wonder-Book, which had only two or three more pages left for the Rhyme-Elves to fill, was open at a new page, with a new poem and a picture of Sylvia seven years ago, coming down between the stars on her crescent moon-boat to be born.

And when she climbed into her mother's bed, and her mother had given her a special birthday kiss, and Sylvia had thanked her for the beautiful new Wonder-Book, this was the poem her mother read to her out of the old one:

Sylvia is seven years old today.
Seven years ago a rainbow shell
Left the full moon, to sail away
And bring her down on Earth to dwell.
Now she is seven a silver bell
Calls back her moon-boat to the skies;
But Sylvia on the Earth must stay,
And in the ways of Earth grow wise.
Sylvia is seven years old today.

Sylvia is seven years old today.
Seven years ago a rosy star,
Her radiant name writ on its ray,
Warmed her most sweetly from afar.
Now she is seven it leaps the bar
Of the blue airy realms, below
To light for her her earthly way

And guide her where she ought to go.
Sylvia is seven years old today.

Sylvia is seven years old today.
Seven years ago twelve fairies stood
Circling the cradle where she lay,
And blessed her sleep, and said she should
Be true and beautiful and good.
Now she is seven their magic ring
Encloses her again, and they
Fresh fairy graces to her bring.
Sylvia is seven years old today.

Sylvia's Birthday

The snow sparkled and the sun shone for Sylvia's birthday. All morning she was happy and busy, helping her mother to prepare for her birthday party; and early in the afternoon Blackbird came *clop — clop — clopping* from the village, with the Old Woodsman walking beside her in his Sunday suit, and with the log-cart piled with children.

Round Sylvia's place at the table there were fir-branches spread, and under these the Old Woodsman and Joan and Terry and Rosaleen and Margaret and Stephen and Luke all quietly hid their birthday gifts. Round everybody else's place were holly leaves and berries in shining trails of tinsel, and coloured candles in gilded acorn and beech-nut moon and star candle-holders, and little bowls of marzipan cherries and strawberries which Sylvia had helped her mother to colour and model. And in the middle of the table stood the big birthday cake which Sylvia had also helped to make, covered with white icing, with seven coloured candles on the top.

When the lights had been turned off, and Sylvia had lit the seven candles on the cake, and Joan and Terry and Rosaleen and Margaret and Stephen and Luke and the Old Woodsman and Sylvia's mother had lit the coloured candles round their plates, they all sat down at the table, and watched Sylvia finding their presents among the fir-branches. And each time she said "Oh!" with delight, all round the table the other children's faces glowed, and their eyes lit up with pleasure each time Sylvia's did.

And after tea they lit the candles on the Christmas tree and sang carols; and then they played games — noisy ones and quiet ones, running-about ones and sitting-still ones;

and then they asked each other riddles and told each other stories.

Then, because it was New Year's Eve, the Old Woodsman showed them a game which country children used to play that night when he was a boy. In an old ladle with a long handle he melted a little lead over the log fire, then poured the melted lead into a bowl of cold water; and it cooled into a new shape, and the Old Woodsman picked it up and showed it them and asked:

"What does it look like?"

And all the children shouted together:

"A boat!"

And the Old Woodsman said:

"That must be the boat that is bringing Peter across the sea."

And he told them about Peter, his little grandson, who was just about their age; and how he had lived in a great city, and was too tall and too thin and too pale and too clever; and so he and his mother were coming to live in the woods with the Old Woodsman, so that the trees and the flowers and the birds and the animals and Sylvia and the other children could help him to get well. And tomorrow Blackbird and the Old Woodsman were meeting Peter's boat and bringing Peter and Peter's mother home.

And Sylvia was so excited at the thought of Peter that it seemed like an extra birthday gift that the kind world was giving her.

Then Joan and Terry and Rosaleen and Margaret and Stephen and Luke each in turn melted a little lead in the ladle with the Old Woodsman's help; and everyone laughed a lot as they guessed what each shape was and what it meant was going to happen in the New Year. And when it came to Sylvia's turn and she held up her odd little lump of lead for everyone to see, everyone shouted, laughing:

"A tooth! Sylvia's is a tooth!"

And the Old Woodsman added:

"Ah, that's a very special tooth, with three New Year gifts for Sylvia!"

And Sylvia remembered her mother telling her on Christmas morning that the Elf-Prince Frey would have three wonderful gifts for her when her first tooth came out; and she felt more excited than ever. And she tickled her loose tooth with her tongue; and it seemed to her that it really was getting shakier.

Then at last it was time to finish the party; and Joan and Terry and Rosaleen and Margaret and Stephen and Luke collected the treasures they had been given from Sylvia's Christmas tree, and said thank-you and good-bye; and the Old Woodsman packed them all into the log-cart; and away went Blackbird, *clop — clop — clopping* back towards the village, taking them all home, tired and happy, to their waiting mothers.

And Sylvia, too, was so tired and happy that she could hardly keep awake long enough to undress and be tucked into bed with all her new birthday toys. But after her mother had tiptoed out and softly closed the door, it seemed suddenly to Sylvia that someone else was in the room; and when she turned her sleepy head to look, there in the moonlight beside her bed stood Sister-in-the-Bushes.

And Sister-in-the-Bushes bent down and smiled and whispered:

"I've come to bring you my birthday present, Sylvia; but you'll think it a very funny one. Open your mouth!"

And she took Sylvia's hand in hers, and guided it to the shaky tooth, and closed Sylvia's thumb and finger on it; and there was a tiny tug and a tiny pang, and there lay the tooth in Sylvia's palm!

And Sylvia gulped:

"It *does* seem *rather* a funny present, Sister-in-the-Bushes!"

140

And Sister-in-the-Bushes smiled again, and whispered:

"I know; but just put it under your pillow, Sylvia, and see what it will bring you!"

So Sylvia sleepily put the tooth under her pillow; and when she looked up again, Sister-in-the-Bushes was no longer there.

And Sylvia thought dreamily:

"I wonder what it *will* bring me? Anyway, *now* I can go to school!"

And with the tip of her tongue she touched the gap where the tooth had been, and thought how funny it felt, and how lovely it would be to go to school, and how wonderful to have Peter for a playmate, and to have Blackbird and the Old Woodsman to take them both to school each day; and then she didn't think anything more, because the next moment she was sound asleep.

Sylvia and the Three Fairies

Sylvia did not know how long she had been asleep when she heard little crows of delight, and tiny voices crying:

"Isn't she beautiful? Oh, *isn't* she beautiful? By sun and moon and stars, *how* beautiful she is!"

Sylvia opened her eyes; and there, about her bed, watching her with looks and cries of joy, were three fairies.

One was a little knight in radiant armour; so Sylvia knew he was an earth-fairy. And one had a fish's tail, like a tiny mermaid; so Sylvia knew she was a water-fairy. And one had wings; so Sylvia knew she was an air-fairy.

And the earth-fairy was reining in his fairy steed under the shelter of a dandelion-plant; and the water-fairy was floating in the white blossom of a water-lily; and the air-fairy was hovering over a mauve meadow-vetchling, alighting every now and then on its topmost wing-shaped flower.

When they saw Sylvia's eyes were open, the earth-knight said:

"Beautiful Sylvia, I am Gnome. And *how* beautiful you are!"

And the water-fairy said:

"Beautiful Sylvia, I am Undine. And *how* beautiful you are!"

And the air-fairy said:

"Beautiful Sylvia, I am Sylph. And *how* beautiful you are!"

And Sylvia said:

"Yes, I remember you all. You showed me how a fairy tree is made. But you couldn't see me then. How is it you can now?"

Then Gnome explained:

"We can see you now because tonight you are seven years old and your first tooth has come out. When little human children lose their first tooth, it is a wonderful moment for fairies!"

And Undine added:

"Yes, till then we couldn't see the little child; and then, in a moment, there he suddenly is, so very beautiful that we think there is nothing so lovely in the whole wide world!"

And Sylvia asked:

"But how did you know about my tooth coming out tonight?"

And Sylph explained:

"Sister-in-the-Bushes told us she had just helped it out, and asked us to come straight to you. She is very anxious you should choose the right tooth-gifts at the palace of Prince Frey; and if you will give your tooth to Gnome, it will help us to help you to choose rightly."

Then Sylvia gladly felt under her pillow, and pulled out her little gleaming tooth, and gave it to Gnome.

And Gnome asked his dandelion:

"Now what shall Sylvia's tooth-gifts be?"

And Undine asked her water-lily:

"Now what shall Sylvia's tooth-gifts be?"

And Sylph asked her meadow-vetchling:

"Now what shall Sylvia's tooth-gifts be?"

Gnome listened for a moment, then said in his hearty, shouting little voice:

"I speak for Earth. Earth's rarest tooth-gift is a winged white horse. It would carry Sylvia to the clouds and back again. Choose this gift, Sylvia."

Undine listened for a moment, then said in her gentle, dreaming voice:

"I speak for Dew. Dew's fairest tooth-gift is a fairy fruit-tree. Every night it bears a fairy peach and a fairy pear; and if Sylvia eats them they will keep her strong and beautiful. Choose this gift, Sylvia."

Sylph listened for a moment, then said in her delicate singing voice:

"I speak for Wind. Wind's noblest tooth-gift is a golden key. It will unlock the richest treasure-chests in Prince Frey's palace, and fill Sylvia's heart with loving understanding. Choose this gift, Sylvia."

Then Gnome and Sylph and Undine said together:

"When the snow-bird comes for you, Sylvia, the tooth-gifts will be waiting. But be sure you choose the right ones!"

Then Gnome, with his fairy steed and his yellow dandelion, and Undine, with her white water-lily, and Sylph, with her mauve meadow-vetchling, disappeared in the twinkling of an eye.

And in the twinkling of another eye, Sylvia was sound asleep again.

The Poem of the Three Tooth-Gifts

When Sylvia woke again at the proper time, she at once remembered Gnome and Sylph and Undine; and she wondered:

"Were they *really* here? Or did I dream them?"

Then she remembered about her tooth coming out. She could feel its little gap with the tip of her tongue, so she knew that *that* had happened, anyway. And she remembered that she had put the tooth under her pillow, and had given it afterwards to Gnome. So she searched under her pillow; but she could not find it anywhere.

So next she turned to her bedside table, in case she had put it there. And there she saw her Wonder-Book, open at a new page — the last page but one — and on the page was a new poem, and by the poem a new picture. And as soon as Sylvia saw the picture, she knew that Gnome and Sylph and Undine had really happened, for it showed Sylvia in bed, and Gnome on his fairy steed beside the yellow dandelion, and Undine floating in her white water-lily, and Sylph hovering over her mauve meadow-vetchling.

So she jumped out of bed and ran with her Wonder-Book to her mother's room. And they wished each other a Very Happy New Year. Then Sylvia told her mother about her first tooth coming out, and smiled widely so that her mother could see the little gap it had left. And her mother gave her a special hug and a silver sixpence, because her first tooth had come out.

Then Sylvia's mother read the new poem in the Wonder-Book; and as Sylvia listened she knew all over again that Gnome and Sylph and Undine had really happened; for this is what the poem said:

What shall Sylvia's tooth-gifts be —
Rare gifts for Sylvia?
About her bed came fairies three,
With Earth's and Wind's and Water's flower;
And pondered what enchanted power
Each should choose for Sylvia's dower.
What shall Sylvia's tooth-gifts be —
Fair gifts for Sylvia?

Shouted Gnome right heartily:
"This shall Sylvia's tooth-gift be —
Earth's gift for Sylvia:
A winged and magic horse shall she
Have to take her from Earth's plain
To the clouds and back again —
A white mare with a golden mane!
This shall be her dower from me —
Earth's gift for Sylvia."

Undine murmured dreamily:
"This shall Sylvia's tooth-gift be —
Dew's gift for Sylvia.
She shall have a fairy tree
Which every night for her shall bear
A fairy peach and a fairy pear,
To eat to keep her strong and fair.
This shall be her dower from me —
Dew's gift for Sylvia."

Then sang Sylph melodiously:
"This shall Sylvia's tooth-gift be —
Wind's gift for Sylvia:
She shall have a golden key
Which shall unlock each chest and door
Of Elfland's richest treasure-store,

And load her heart with loving lore.
This shall be her dower from me —
Wind's gift for Sylvia."

So these shall Sylvia's tooth-gifts be —
Rare gifts for Sylvia.
A wonder-filled New Year starts she
With a white winged horse, and a golden key,
And a peach and a pear on a fairy tree,
And a fairy benedicite —
Rare tooth-gifts from the fairies three —
Fair gifts for Sylvia!

Sylvia and the Elf-Prince Frey

Sylvia's mother had only just finished reading the Poem of the Three Tooth-gifts when, early in the morning though it still was, they heard Blackbird *clop — clop — clopping* along the woodland path. So Sylvia jumped out of her mother's bed, and ran to the casement window and opened it, and knelt with her breath melting the ice-ferns which the frost-fairies had painted on the glass during the night, while she called:

"A Happy New Year, Blackbird! A Happy New Year, Mr Woodsman!"

The Old Woodsman was wearing his Sunday suit and his tall starched collar and his stiff hat; and he called back to her:

"A Happy New Year to you, too, Sylvia! Blackbird and I are on our way to meet Peter and his mother. First thing tomorrow morning I'll bring him here to you!"

And Sylvia breathed whole banks of ice-ferns off the window in her excitement, and leaned right out to show the Old Woodsman the gap her tooth had left; and he was tremendously impressed. And he said:

"That means you'll be going to the palace of Prince Frey tonight for your tooth-gifts, Sylvia."

And Sylvia asked, a little anxiously:

"You don't think he'll forget to send his snow-bird? I shan't know how to get there if he does."

And the Old Woodsman answered comfortingly:

"Oh no, he never forgets."

When Blackbird had gone *clop — clop — clopping* away, Sylvia ran downstairs to her toy-cupboard, and brought out the snow-bird the Old Woodsman had given her for

Christmas; and all through the day she carried it about with her, wondering about all the wonderful things which would happen when the fairy snow-bird came; and at bedtime she took it to bed with her.

And so it seemed quite natural, after she had gone to sleep that night, that she should feel something soft and warm and downy brushing her cheek, and that when she opened her eyes there should be a beautiful white snow-bird nestling on her pillow and brushing her cheek with his wing.

As soon as the snow-bird saw Sylvia was awake, he piped:

"Take hold of my golden ribbon, Sylvia! I have come to take you to the palace of Prince Frey!"

And as soon as Sylvia had grasped the end of the golden ribbon that was round the snow-bird's throat, she found herself floating in the air and looking down at a shining little garden on her bed.

She felt a pricking in her heels; and when she turned and looked, she saw that each heel had grown a tiny wing. So she half-flew, half-floated, drawn through the air by the snow-bird, till they came towards a forest. And the snow-bird piped:

"That is a magic forest, Sylvia, and there are two ways of reaching it — one across that narrow river of pitch, and one across this wide, wide river of starlight. Which way would you like to go?"

And Sylvia looked down at them — the narrow river of pitch so black and ugly, the wide, wide river of starlight so beautiful and sparkling — and she answered:

"Oh, Snow-bird, the wide, wide river of starlight, please!"

And the snow-bird piped back:

"I am glad you chose the river of starlight, Sylvia. The river of pitch is narrower, but it is harder to cross, for it drags little children's feet down into it, and clogs their wings, so that they cannot fly. And on the other side of the river of pitch the Black Huntsman lies in wait, and hunts the children who choose that way; and if he hunts them into his iron stove they can only get out if somebody outside helps them."

So the snow-bird and Sylvia flew across the wide, wide river of starlight and came to the magic forest; and as they flew over the tops of the trees, Sylvia heard a voice crying faintly far below:

"Let me out! Let me out!"

And Sylvia pleaded:

"Dear Snow-bird, couldn't we stop and see if we can help?"

So the snow-bird folded her white wings, and she and Sylvia sank slowly down into the magic forest.

And all the time the voice, very angry and frightened, kept crying:

"Let me out! Let me out!"

Sylvia ran between the trees towards it; and there, in a clearing in the forest, she came to an iron stove; and the angry, frightened voice came from inside the iron stove.

And Sylvia turned and turned the handle, and shook the door and banged the door and pushed the door and leaned on the door; but the door remained fast closed.

Then the voice called to her from inside the iron stove:

"The only way is to *scrape* a way through. You scrape from your side and I'll scrape from mine."

And Sylvia scraped till her finger-tips were sore; and at last a tiny hole appeared. And at once the door flew open; and out came a little boy. He looked the same age as Sylvia, but he was taller and thinner and paler, and the tiny wings on his heels were clogged with pitch.

And the little boy thanked her, and said:

"The Black Huntsman hunted me into this iron stove

when I was on the way to the palace of Prince Frey to get my tooth-gifts."

And Sylvia exclaimed:

"That's where we're going — let's go together!"

But when they took the snow-bird's golden ribbon in their hands and tried to fly, they found that the little boy's wings were too heavily clogged with pitch; so they walked the rest of the way through the magic forest, with the snow-bird fluttering ahead to show them the right path.

And at the edge of the magic forest, the most beautiful fairy prince in the whole world came to meet them, and welcomed them into a wonderful palace fashioned of snow. He led them from room to room, and every room was gay with flowers and filled with treasures; and the fairy prince said kindly:

"Come as often as you like to roam through my palace and explore its treasures!"

Then the pale little boy said that he felt thirsty. So the Elf-Prince Frey brought golden bowls of wine and milk; and he said to the two children:

"Choose whichever you like to drink."

And the pale little boy said at once:

"Milk is only for babies. *I* shall choose wine, like the grown-ups do. *You* choose wine, too, Sylvia!"

And he took a bowl of the wine, and began to drink it.

This made Sylvia feel a little ashamed of really liking milk best; and she was just stretching out her hand to take a bowl of the wine when a soft voice whispered in her ear:

"Choose the milk, Sylvia! Wine is only for grown-ups."

And glancing round, Sylvia caught a glimpse of Sister-in-the-Bushes standing lovingly beside her.

So Sylvia took the milk; and with every sip she could see in the crystal mirrors on the walls that she grew more rosy and beautiful. But when she looked at the little boy, she saw that with every sip he took of the wine he grew still taller and thinner and paler.

When Sylvia had drunk the last drop of her milk, she saw that a small golden key lay at the bottom of the bowl. And when the pale little boy had drunk the last drop of his wine, he saw at the bottom of *his* bowl a small key made of lead. Then both children knew they had received the first of their tooth-gifts.

And they ran excitedly about the room, opening with their keys the big treasure-chests which were ranged along the walls. And always Sylvia's golden key unlocked chests of gold and pearls and beautiful things and pictures. And always the pale little boy's key of lead unlocked chests of scissors and knives and compasses and things which grown-ups use.

To Sylvia the strange thing was that the pale little boy was just as delighted with the treasures his key of lead unlocked as she was with the treasures her golden key unlocked.

And she said to the Elf-Prince Frey:

"It doesn't seem fair — I have all the nicest things! Couldn't I lend my golden key to the pale little boy?"

And Prince Frey said, smiling kindly:

"You can't *lend* it to him, Sylvia, because it will open the treasure-chests only for you. But what you *can* do is to share your treasures with him."

Then the Elf-Prince Frey took the two children into his orchard, in which grew every sort of fruit tree in the world.

And he said to them:

"For your second tooth-gift you may each of you choose a fruit-tree to be your very own."

Then the pale little boy ran to an apple-tree loaded with apples, and cried:

"I shall choose this! You choose an apple-tree, too, Sylvia!"

This made Sylvia feel she ought to; and she was just going to when a soft voice whispered in her ear:

"Choose the tree Undine promised you, Sylvia."

And glancing round, Sylvia caught a glimpse of Sister-in-the-Bushes standing lovingly beside her.

So Sylvia choose a tree which bore a fairy peach and a fairy pear. And when she bit the fairy peach she felt strong; and when she bit the fairy pear the little gap in her teeth stopped bothering her and her finger-tips stopped feeling sore from scraping the iron stove. But when the pale little boy bit his apple, he grew thinner and taller and paler.

And Sylvia felt sorry for him, and she said to the Elf-Prince Frey:

"It doesn't seem fair — I have all the nicest things! Couldn't I lend my fairy tree to the pale little boy?"

And Prince Frey said, smiling kindly:

"You can't *lend* it to him, Sylvia, because it will bear its fairy fruit only for you. But what you *can* do is to share its fruit with him."

Then the Elf-Prince Frey took the two children into his meadow, where many horses, some black, some white, were feeding.

And he said to them:

"For your third tooth-gift you may each of you choose a horse for your very own."

And the two children ran to and fro in great excitement, looking at all the horses and wondering which to choose. And they saw that the black horses were very clever, and could count and nod their heads in answer to questions; but the white horses stood quite still and fed quietly, except that every now and again one would strike the ground with his hoof, and then a spring of clear, sweet water would come bubbling out.

Then the pale little boy went up to a black horse, and put his hand on it, and cried:

"I shall choose this one! You choose a black one, too, Sylvia! Just think of having a clever horse who can count and answer questions!"

This made Sylvia think that after all that *would* be something rather special; and she was just about to lay her hand on a black horse, too, when a soft voice whispered in her ear:

"Choose the horse Gnome promised you, Sylvia."

And glancing round, Sylvia caught a glimpse of Sister-in-the-Bushes standing lovingly beside her.

So Sylvia looked at all the white horses, but none of them had wings. But just then one lifted its head and looked at her; and Sylvia loved it there and then, and went to it and laid her hand upon its back.

And at once she felt herself rising, rising, rising in the air, riding the white horse; and her hair was growing longer and more brightly golden, and streaming out behind her; and the white mane of the horse was growing longer, too, and streaming out behind; and the long white mane and the long golden hair mingled, and together they turned into white and golden wings.

To be riding like this high above the world on her winged white horse was more wonderful than anything Sylvia had ever known. As she leaned and looked below, she saw the strong, kind Earth patiently carrying men and women and children and animals, and stones valiantly helping the Earth to bear their weight. And though it was mid-winter, in the kingdom of Prince Frey she could see all the seasons working — the spring saps rising in the plants to greet the moon; and the warm sunbeams drawing up the tall green cornstalks; and the winds and the bees and the butterflies carrying pollen from flower to flower; and the flowers distilling honey.

And in the cornfields she saw birds and animals and earthworms all helping the wheat to grow, and fairies kneading dew and rain and starlight into grain. And everywhere that Prince Frey went, the corn sprang up to meet his smile, and tiny loaves clustered at the top of each corn-stalk till it looked like a fairy tree bearing a harvest of fairy bread.

And Sylvia was filled with thankfulness to Earth and stone and sun and moon and wind and bee and butterfly and bird and beast and worm and flower and fairy and the Elf-Prince Frey himself.

And there below, also, Sylvia could see the pale little boy watching his black horse count, quite happy with his choice. But Sylvia was sad for him, because although that might be clever, he was missing all these wonders one could only see from high above the world.

And she called down to the Elf-Prince Frey:

"It doesn't seem fair — I have all the nicest things! Couldn't I lend my winged white horse to the pale little boy?"

And Prince Frey smiled up at her, and said kindly:

"You can't *lend* it to him, Sylvia, because it will soar to the clouds only for you. But what you *can* do is to take him up with you sometimes."

And then a trumpet sounded; and the winged white horse carried Sylvia swiftly away; and soon, there below, she again saw the little shining garden on her bed. And the white horse sank slowly down; and the white and golden wings turned back into white mane and golden hair; and before Sylvia knew it, she was back inside the little garden and was thinking drowsily:

"That trumpet is Mother's cockerel crowing!"

And then she was fast asleep.

The Poem of the Fairy Bread

When Sylvia woke again, it was again to feel something soft and warm and downy brushing her cheek; and when she turned her head, there once more was a beautiful white snow-bird nestling on her pillow. At first she thought she must be dreaming last night all over again, till she saw that round this snow-bird's throat there was no golden ribbon; and then she knew that it was not the snow-bird of the Elf-Prince Frey this time, but her own snow-bird which the Old Woodsman had made for her from feathers from the wood.

And when she turned to look at her Wonder-Book, again she saw a snow-bird; for the Wonder-Book was open at a new page, and on the page was a new poem, and beside the poem was a picture of herself and the little boy she had rescued from the iron stove being guided through the magic forest by the snow-bird of Prince Frey. And when she picked up the Wonder-Book to look at the picture more closely, she saw that this page was the very last page of all.

So when she took the book into her mother's bed, she said:

"Mother, I feel solemn. This is the Rhyme-Elves' last poem in *this* Wonder-Book. But they *will* go on painting poems in my new one, won't they, Mother?"

And her mother answered:

"Yes, if you go on being grateful to them, Sylvia. And now that you have a winged white horse, they'll help you to bring back your own poems from the clouds, as well."

Then they looked back through the full Wonder-Book together — laughing at Lordly Cock and Hugin's turnip, and remembering with joy the Youngest Prince, and the

star-princess Helia, and the kind Cordita, and Knight
Michael.

And then Sylvia's mother read the last poem in the
Wonder-Book; and this was it:

Thank you, Earth beneath my feet;
Thank you, stones that keep Earth firm;
Flowers, that work to make food sweet;
Every bird and beast and worm
Which helps the soil bring forth the wheat;
And fairies, kneading dew and rain
And starlight into glowing grain.
Fairy trees bear fairy bread,
That elves and children may be fed.

Thank you, Sun, that from the skies
Makes the tall green corn-stalks grow;
Winds and bees and butterflies,
Ferrying pollen to and fro;
Moon, that makes the spring saps rise;
Frey, whose warming smile can cause
Golden loaves to spring from straws.
Fairy trees bear fairy bread,
That elves and children may be fed.

Sylvia and Peter

Sylvia was finishing dressing after listening to the Poem
of the Fairy Bread when she heard Blackbird *clop — clop
— clopping* along the woodland path. She had just time to
comb out the tangles in her curls, and to put on the proper
velvet hair-ribbon from the box St Nicholas had given her,
before she heard the Old Woodsman's slow, crunching step

on the snow. She climbed up on to the window-seat to open her bedroom window; and the Old Woodsman turned up his kind, wise old face, and called:

"Good-morning, Sylvia! I've brought you Peter!"

And when Sylvia looked at the little boy beside him, the little grandson who was too pale and too tall and too thin and too clever, she cried "Oh!"; for who should it be but the pale little boy she had been with all night in the kingdom of Prince Frey!

And when Peter looked up and saw Sylvia, he cried "Oh!", too. And they smiled at each other; and already they felt friends.

And as Sylvia jumped down from the window-seat, her feet went hop-skip-and-jump, and her happiness bubbled up into a little song:

"Oh, how lovely it is to be seven years old, and to have given your first tooth to the fairies!"

"Oh, how lovely it is to be starting school next week!"

"Oh, how lovely it is to have Prince Frey for your friend, and his palace to roam in!"

"Oh, how lovely it is to have a winged white horse and a golden key and a fairy fruit-tree and a Peter to share them with!"

"What a beautiful new New Year!"

And Sylvia ran beaming downstairs to join Peter.

GOODBYE, SYLVIA — JUST FOR NOW